Great Register

of

El Dorado County, California, 1867,

With the

Supplemental List of 1868

D. W. Standeford
El Dorado County Clerk

JANAWAY PUBLISHING
Santa Maria, California

> ### *Notice*
> This book is rare and extremely difficult to locate. Because of their rarity, it was necessary to have the original images, which were contained on microfilm, digitized for printing, often resulting in imperfect print, and leaving the impression of over-inking. Also, in many older books, foxing (or discoloration) occurs and, in some instances, print lightens with wear and age. Reprinted books, such as this, often duplicate these flaws, notwithstanding efforts to reduce or eliminate them. The pages of this reprint have been digitally enhanced and, where possible, the flaws eliminated in order to provide clarity of content and a pleasant reading experience.

Great Register of El Dorado County [California] 1867.
With the
Supplemental List of 1868.

Originally published
Placerville, California
1867

Reprinted by:

Janaway Publishing, Inc.
732 Kelsey Ct.
Santa Maria, California 93454
(805) 925-1038
www.JanawayPublishing.com

2004, 2017

ISBN: 978-0-9741957-8-0

Made in the United States of America

INTRODUCTION

During the last-half of the 1800s, each California County periodically produced their "Great Register," as required by legislation, and which published the County Voter Registration List for the specified period. At election time, published copies of these books were given to local precincts to verify voter registration, and, following the election, most books were discarded or destroyed. The individual County Clerks of each county certified the publications as 'true and complete.'

El Dorado County, California, was in the heart of 'Gold Country,' during the great Gold Rush of 1849. Thousands of individuals, from all over the United States, descended upon this area in search of their fortune, and many remained following the bust. This 1867 Voter Registration for El Dorado County is a valuable resource for local historians and genealogists. The information it contains includes the names, ages, place of nativity, occupation, and place of residence of each registered voter in the County, and totals approximately 5,000 individuals. Although arranged by the letters of the alphabet, it is not an alphabetical listing. If the surname begins with the letter "A", it will be listed on those pages beginning with that letter, but you may have to search through the pages to locate the person for whom you are looking.

This book is rare and extremely difficult to locate. Because of their rarity, it was necessary to have the original images, which were contained on microfilm, digitized for printing, often resulting in imperfect print, and leaving the impression of over-inking. Books reprinted from this method, often duplicate these flaws and others, notwithstanding efforts to reduce or eliminate them. The pages of this reprint have been digitally enhanced and, where possible, the flaws eliminated in order to provide clarity of content and a pleasant reading experience.

Janaway Publishing, Inc.
July 2004

GREAT REGISTER

1867.
and Supplemental List of 1868.
El Dorado County.

COURIER PRINT, PLACERVILLE.
1867.

Great Register, El Dorado County.

[A]

NAME.	Age	Place of Nativity.	Occupation.	Local Residence.
Arnold, George W.	22	New Jersey	Farmer	White Oak, Green Val.
Alter, Henry	23	Ohio	"	" " Deer Creek.
Anzoh, Damirus	33	Switzerland	Miner	Placerville, 3d Ward.
Avidsson, Charles John	48	Sweden	Jeweler	" 2d Ward.
Andrews, Edward	33	Pennsylvania	Tinsmith	" 1st Ward.
Anderson, James Madison	37	Pennsylvania	Miner	" 4th Ward.
Adams, John Quinsey	28	Ohio	"	" 3d Ward.
Alsbourg, Sigmund	39	Germany	Merchant	" 3d Ward.
Ansley, Staydll	38	Pennsylvania	Laborer	" Township.
Averill, Franklin	29	Maine	Wagon Maker	" 1st Ward.
Alverson, Stephen Henry	25	Illinois	Blacksmith	" 1st Ward.
Ackley, Ezra	34	Maine	Carriage Maker	" 1st Ward.
Alter, Simon	52	Pennsylvania	Water Agent	" 2d Ward.
Allen, John Page	40	Maine	Miner	" 4th Ward.
Albex, Andrew	31	Kentucky	Farmer	Blakeley, Placerville.
Arnold, John Milton	59	New York	Coroner	Green Val., White Oak.
Ardery, James	62	Great Britain	Laborer	Placerville, 2d Ward.
Altaffer, George	38	Ohio	Farmer	Clarksville, White Oak.
Allhoff, Martin	39	Prussia	Vine Grower	Coloma.
Ames, Nathaniel Oren	42	Maine	Miner	Placerville, 1st Ward.
Adams, Albert	30	Kentucky	Farmer	Blakely, Placerville.
Anderson, Thomas	34	Great Britain	Miner	Placerville.
Arnold, William	37	Great Britain	"	" Smith's Flat.
Allbright Charles	39	Hanover	"	"
Arvington, And'w Jack'n	36	Ohio	Toll Collector	"
Armstrong, Wm. Henry	25	Illinois	Farmer	" 4th Ward.
Anderson, James	31	Ohio	"	Kelsey.
Askew, James	35	England	Laborer	Mud Springs.
Aldrich, Wm. Burlingame	46	Rhode Island	Farmer	Coloma, Cold Springs.
Adams, James Ross	35	Missouri	"	Cosumnes, Coyote.
Adams, George McKay	40	New Jersey	Miner	Diamond Springs.
Amidon, Charles Lyon	50	New Jersey	Farmer	" "
Agren, Hans Urick	44	Sweden	Miner	Placerville Township.
Adkins, Charles	34	Alabama	"	Diamond Springs.
Allen, Edward	41	England	Shoemaker	Mud Springs.
Angus, John	51	Scotland	Farmer	Kelsey.
Ash, Robert Walter	36	Pennsylvania	Miner	Georgetown.
Ashton, John	42	Pennsylvania	Barkeeper	"
Abby, Albert Thomas	45	New York	Miner	"
Ayer, Cephas	28	Maine	Hostler	Lake Valley.
Anible, John Wesley	41	Kentucky	Farmer	Gold Hill.
Armstrong, John Willard	46	Delaware	Blacksmith	Kelsey.
Aliphin, Luke Prior	76	Virginia	Farmer	"
Anderson William Cory	35	New Jersey	Miner	"
Adams, William	40	Kentucky	Hotel Keeper	Diamond Springs.
Askew, William Meigs	36	Georgia	Miner	Cosumnes.

NAME.	Age	Place of Nativity.	Occupation.	Local Residence.
Arnfield, Allen Hamblet'n	44	North Carolina	Farmer	Cosumnes.
Anderson, Daniel	71	Massachusetts	"	Greenwood.
Ashley, Wm. Emory	34	Massachusetts	Blacksmith	"
Ayers, James Milton	28	Tennessee	Laborer	Shingle Springs.
Adams, Emanuel	33	Pennsylvania	Miner	Spanish Camp.
Avery, Geo. Washington	31	Missouri	"	Latrobe.
Atwood, Solomon Louis	30	Maine	Teamster	Buckeye Flat.
Allen, Thomas	46	Ireland	Saloon-keeper	Kelsey.
Alexander, Horatio	36	Maine	Miner	Placerville.
Atmore, Richard	36	England	Farmer	Mud Springs.
Abbott, Charles Eliot	43	N. Hampshire	Miner	White Oak.
Anderson, Larkin	38	South Carolina	"	Georgetown.
Adkins, Jessey	40	Kentucky	Ditch Agent	"
Adams, Henry Bellews	30	Massachusetts	Carpenter	Kelsey.
Anderson, Jeremiah S	45	Upper Canada	Miner	Georgetown.
Armstrong, Thomas "Z"	36	Ireland	"	"
Adkins, John	44	England	"	
Anderson, Siver	47	Norway	"	Greenwood.
Andrews, Amund	38	Norway	"	
Agon, Thomas	47	Ireland	"	Salmon Falls.
Anderson, John	43	Sweden	"	Mud Springs.
Atherton, Felmer	44	Great Britain	"	Placerville Township.
Ames, Frank William	31	N. Hampshire	Engineer	Diamond Springs.
Avansion, Nicholas	22	Italy	Laborer	Placerville, 4th Ward.
Aul, James Ross	23	Missouri	Clerk	Lake Valley.
Alt, Peter	44	Darmstadt	Merchant	Cosumnes Township.
Anderson, James	53	Scotland	Miner	Mud Springs.
Ardery, George	30	Ireland	Teamster	Placerville, 3d Ward.
Arnold, Gottlieb D	35	Prussia	Miner	Mud Springs.
Art, Peter	51	Germany	"	" "
Antonio, John	34	Russia	"	Placerville.
Anderson, William	47	Great Britain	Farmer	Coloma.
Antonille, Vincent	37	Italy	Miner	Greenwood.
Ackley, Hiram Roderick	33	Connecticut	"	Georgetown.
Andrew, James Louis	54	North Carolina	Cabinet-maker	"
Allen, George Wiman	29	Maine	Confectioner	"
Abbey, Thomas Albert	45	New York	Miner	"
Anderson, George	34	Great Britain	"	Placerville.
Allen, Thos. Jefferson	36	Virginia	"	Diamond Springs.
Appleby, Charles	33	New Jersey	"	" "
Alet, Chas. Frederick	37	New York	"	Gold Hill, Coloma.
Akin, William	32	Ohio	"	Cold Springs.
Adams, Andrew Jackson	35	Pennsylvania	Merchant	Latrobe.
Armstrong, Alex. Steel	27	Pennsylvania	Miner	White Oak.
Allen, Harry Session	51	Massachusetts	"	Placerville.
Arnes, Jacob	44	Prussia	"	Indian Diggings.
Ayers, Stephen	71	Virginia	"	Mount Gregory.
Angell, Jonathan	26	Rhode Island	"	White Oak Township.
Alden, Saml. Jemmison	35	Indiana	Druggist	Georgetown.
Allen, Jacob	41	Massachusetts	Farmer	Salmon Falls.
Adams, John	56	Pennsylvania	Teamster	Shingle Springs.
Allen, Thomas	47	Ireland	Farmer	Placerville Township.
Anderson, Toor	24	Norway	Miner	Georgetown.

B

NAME.	Age	Place of Nativity.	Occupation.	Local Residence.
Blanchard, Geo. Granv'lle	41	New York	Lawyer	Placerville, 2d Ward.
Blakely, Hiram Edward	27	Pennsylvania	Farmer	Deer Creek, White Oak.
Bennett, Erasmus Darwin	23	Illinois	"	" " " "
Bennett, Eben	42	New York	"	" " " "
Beaver, John	69	New York	Miner	Clarksville, " "
Bates, Ashley Beauford	39	South Carolina	Lawyer	" " " "
Bean, Russell Thomas	41	Tennessee	Blacksmith	" " " "
Bence, Dennis Phillips	40	Indiana	Farmer	" " " "

NAME.	Age	Place of Nativity.	Occupation.	Local Residence.
Bachelor, John	34	Indiana	Miner	Deer Valley, White Oak.
Brace, Marvin Shulds	30	Indiana	Saloon-keeper	Placerville.
Bye, Frank William	38	Ohio	Miner	" 1st Ward.
Brooks, Cornelius Dabney	36	Virginia	Farmer	Diamond Springs.
Bell, William	23	Australia	Saloon-keeper	Placerville, 1st Ward.
Bradley, James Henry	35	Kentucky	Miner	Mountain Township.
Bery, Robert	37	Ireland	"	Coloma.
Brusie, James	41	New York	Clerk	Placerville, 3d Ward.
Broad, Charles	42	England	Miner	"
Brown, Elias	53	New York	"	Coloma.
Bery, Reuben Kelly	52	New York	Farmer	Salmon Falls.
Burns, Archibald	36	New York	"	Mud Springs.
Bartram, Wheeler	58	Connecticut	Millman	Placerville Township.
Burns, Thomas	43	Scotland	Farmer	Mud Springs.
Blackwood, H. Craig	35	North Carolina	Miner	" "
Bryon, John	45	New York	Farmer	" "
Borowsky, Michael	40	Poland	Saloon-keeper	Placerville.
Bomberger, Simon	36	Bavaria	Merchant	"
Bryant, Warren	33	New York	Lumberman	" Township.
Black, Robert Henry	45	Pennsylvania	Hotel-keeper	Placerville, 1st Ward.
Bodfish, Wm. Henry	33	Massachusetts	Lawyer	Coloma.
Brockway, Saml. Henry	43	Vermont	Justice of Peace	"
Barnes, Joshua Lawrence	50	North Carolina	Farmer	"
Booker, Isaac	25	Ohio	"	Uniontown, Coloma.
Beebe, Edwin Orson	39	Ohio	Wagon-maker	" "
Brian, Heinrick	45	Germany	Saloon-keeper	Placerville, 1st Ward.
Bee, Frederick Alonzo	40	New York	Farmer	" "
Bradford, Joseph	35	England	Miner	Gold Hill, Coloma.
Breslin, John	33	Ireland	Farmer	Placerville Township.
Burns, Wm. Scott	49	Ireland	Merchant	" 3d Ward.
Bishop, Francis Augustus	36	Connecticut	Engineer	" 1st Ward.
Brewer, Henry Hemsted	47	New York	Miner	Gold Hill, Coloma.
Brown, Thomas	46	Sweden	Farmer	Coloma.
Baker, Horatio Walker	31	New York	Stage propriet'r	Placerville.
Bullard, John Q. Adams	41	Indiana	Clerk	" 1st Ward.
Biron, Hyman	86	Louisiana	Surgeon	" 3d "
Brown, C. Butterfield	39	Vermont	Farmer	" 3d "
Barnes, Henry	68	Connecticut	Laborer	" 2d "
Barss, Fred. Ferdinand	36	England	Watchmaker	" 2d "
Booth, Geo. Albert	35	Connecticut	Mason	" 3d "
Benner, Nicholaus	28	Prussia	Laborer	" Township.
Bitley, Wm. Henry	73	New York	Miner	" 2d Ward.
Bocholoer, John Godlove	42	Germany	Farmer	" Township.
Brown, William	31	Ohio	Laborer	" "
Barlow, Geo. Washington	31	Pennsylvania	Water Agent	" "
Briggs, Enos Woods	27	Illinois	Miner	" "
Bush, John	61	Massachusetts	Attorney	" 3d Ward.
Bacon, John Hine	37	Massachusetts	Surveyor	" 3d "
Breeze, James Henry	24	Missouri	Harness-maker	" 1st "
Burnham, George	38	Connecticut	Clerk	" 4th "
Boop, John Daniel	34	Pennsylvania	Lumber Mchn't	" 3d "
Bell, Aaron	32	Pennsylvania	Insurance Agt	" 3d "
Baber, Andrew Jackson	37	Ohio	Tax Collector	" 3d "
Bailey, George	30	Ohio	Miner	" Township.
Beebe, Day	31	Pennsylvania	"	" "
Brown, Thomas	37	Pennsylvania	Blacksmith	" "
Bamber, Ira Sabine	46	New York	Farmer	" 1st Ward.
Brewster, Stephen Gay	45	New York	Hotel-keeper	" Township.
Barnaby, Lewis Milton	37	New York	Miner	" 3d Ward.
Baldwin, David	31	Ohio	"	" 3d "
Brandon, Wm. Joseph	33	Illinois	Teamster	" 4th "
Buck, Moses Powers	49	New York	Farmer	" Township.
Barker, Hugh	44	Pennsylvania	Surveyor	" 4th Ward.

NAME.	Age	Place of Nativity.	Occupation.	Local Residence.
Buchan, William	43	Scotland	Merchant	Greenwood Township.
Brown, Washington	43	Pennsylvania	Miner	" "
Baker, John Frank	48	Germany	"	Placerville, 1st Ward.
Blakely, Alburn James	39	Pennsylvania	Farmer	" Township.
Black, Isiah	38	Indiana	Miner	" 2d Ward.
Binswangear, Louis	54	Germany	Farmer	" 3d Ward.
Bates, Cristian	38	Germany	Shoemaker	" 1st Ward.
Burns, Cornelius	40	Ireland	Miner	Diamond Sp. Township
Bowser, George Henry	44	Maryland	Farmer	Placerville, 1st Ward.
Buck, Hiram Marion	29	New York	Engineer	" 3d Ward.
Beckwith, William	34	New York	Teamster	" 4th Ward.
Brown, Samuel Ash	42	Pennsylvania	Merchant	" 5th Ward.
Bronson, James Cathcart	36	Indiana	Clerk	" 5th Ward.
Brewster, Charles Wm	37	New York	Merchant	" 5th Ward.
Bergantz, Jacob	36	France	Miner	Coloma.
Becker, Simon Samuel	34	Pennsylvania	Blacksmith	Placerville, 4th Ward.
Brooks, George	44	Great Britain	Miner	Diamond Springs.
Badger, Samuel Edmund	33	Ohio	"	Placerville, 3d Ward.
Beckman, John	44	Prussia	"	" "
Bothwell, William	51	Ireland	"	Coloma.
Bennett, David	45	Indiana	Farmer	Clarksville.
Bell, John	34	Illinois	Miner	Gold Hill, Coloma T'p.
Behme, Julius Henry	27	Germany	"	" " "
Bennett, John Bell	40	Pennsylvania	Carpenter	Placerville, 3d Ward.
Bayler, Joseph	38	Ohio	Harness maker	" "
Black, James	38	Sweden	Farmer	Salmon Falls.
Bucklin, George Henry	39	Massachusetts	Miner	Placerville, 1st Ward.
Bell, William Johnson	38	Pennsylvania	Teamster	Smith's Flat.
Burnum, John F	50	Holland	Farmer	Chili Ravine, Pl. T'p.
Bennett, Erasmus	24	Illinois	"	Durock, White Oak.
Baker, Adam	42	Holland	Blacksmith	Placerville, 1st Ward.
Brown, George Anthony	36	England	Miner	" 2d Ward.
Baringer, Frederick	34	Germany	Watchmaker	" "
Brown, Thomas Wren	30	Rhode Island	Cook	" "
Briggs, Lewis Madison	26	North Carolina	Miner	White Rock, Pl. T'p.
Berg, Emanuel	39	Bavaria	Merchant	Diamond Springs.
Brockway, Silas Wright	37	New York	District Judge	Placerville.
Bino, Laurenzi	58	Italy	Farmer	Fort Jim, Diamond T'p.
Barnes, Joseph John	40	Kentucky		Coloma.
Brace, Edwin Madison	34	Indiana	Saloonkeeper	Coloma.
Brizse, Norman	38	Missouri	Miner	Uniontown.
Bryant, William Wilder	39	Vermont	Teamster	Gold Hill.
Bates, Walter Chesley	32	Missouri	Farmer	Cosumnes Township.
Burrows, George	26	New Jersey	Miner	" "
Bowman, Daniel	39	New York	Farmer	" "
Barnes, Benjamin Merry	38	Kentucky	Miner	Placerville, 2d Ward.
Bunker, Benjamin Barron	25	New York	Watchman	" 1st Ward.
Brown, Abner Augustus	33	Rhode Island	Tailor	" 2d Ward.
Barnes, James	29	Maryland	Miner	" 3d Ward.
Bennett, Richard Sissel	38	Vermont	Farmer	Smith's Flat.
Bryant, Berkley	37	Ohio	Dairyman	Placerville Township.
Brightman, Henry	35	Massachusetts	Lumberman	" "
Brooks, Henry	33	Germany	Miner	Cosumnes Township.
Brown, Henry W	28	New York	Farmer	Diamond Springs.
Buffington, Jas. Reynolds	42	Pennsylvania	Merchant	" "
Bowles, Obadiah White	36	Kentucky	Ditch Agent	" "
Bragdon, Charles	39	Maine	Farmer	" "
Barney, Albert Coleman	35	Maine	Miner	" "
Balmforth, Ralph	36	England	Stage Prop'r	Georgetown.
Bradbury, Erastus Gros	40	Maine	Miner	Diamond Springs.
Bachnish, August	53	Prussia	Saloonkeeper	Shingle Springs.
Bradshaw, William M	38	Ireland	Merchant	Placerville, 2d Ward.
Brauer, Sebastian	40	Bavaria	Farmer	Georgetown Township.

NAMES.	Age	Place of Nativity.	Occupation.	Local Residence.
Bell, Robert	37	Ireland	Merchant	Coloma.
Boyles, Henry	33	Ohio	Teamster	Mud Springs.
Brown, John	41	Pennsylvania	Miner	"
Bradshaw, Marcus Farner	29	Alabama	Carpenter	Strawberry.
Braston, Solomon Dupee	35	Massachusetts	Express Agent	Placerville.
Bishoff, Frederick	41	Prussia	Saloon Keeper	Shingle Springs.
Bowker, Gideon Fletcher	39	Vermont	Miner	Pleasant Valley.
Bayles, William Harper	30	Ohio	Clerk	Georgetown.
Bowker, David Wheeler	43	New York	Musician	"
Bayless, Canada	36	Ohio	Wheelwright	"
Buck, Addison	32	Kentucky	Carpenter	"
Bryant, Lewis	33	Massachusetts	Miner	"
Bixby, William	52	New York	Farmer	"
Baldwin, Minor Pratt	37	New York	Miner	"
Burk, James	41	Maryland	"	"
Bentley, Seymour	38	New York	"	Garden Valley.
Ballard, Harrison	49	Maine	"	Volcanoville.
Bayless, Yancey	36	South Carolina	"	Empire Cañon.
Barnes, Seward	32	Illinois	Laborer	Strawberry Valley.
Bennett, Elnathan War'n	36	New York	Hotel Keeper	Lake Valley.
Barwell, Judson	23	Illinois	Farmer	Uniontown.
Brown, Thomas Roger	40	New York	Carpenter	Salmon Falls.
Bennett, John	36	Massachusetts	Miner	Kelsey Township.
Banchor, Eli	65	N. Hampshire	"	"
Brown, Sabin	58	Rhode Island	"	"
Bradbury, Theophelus	44	Massachusetts	"	"
Bennett, Peter	71	Connecticut	"	"
Bryant, Joseph	44	New York	Lumberman	Diamond Springs.
Bruce, Marshal Duane	33	New York	Farmer	Coyoteville.
Banks, David Porter	43	Maine	Laborer	"
Bicknell, Charles Coffin	46	Tennessee	Miner	Indian Diggings.
Barney, James L	36	New York	Farmer	"
Bickford, Albion	35	N. Hampshire	"	"
Barney, William	32	Pennsylvania	Miner	Fair Play.
Barnes, Hector	40	New York	"	Indian Diggings
Bates, Samuel Louis	36	Missouri	"	Spanish Creek.
Bates, James Elias	38	Missouri	"	" "
Barney, Joseph	40	New York	Farmer	Perry's "
Bell, Lyman Sylvester	38	New York	Miner	Indian Diggings.
Ballick, John Pee	34	New York	Farmer	Fair Play.
Burnham, Ozro Hill	39	New York	"	Georgetown.
Brown, Silas Witherby	48	Maine	"	Pilot Hill.
Bucknam, Magnus Junson	44	N. Hampshire	Teamster	Spanish Dry Diggings.
Bucknam, Charles Caleb	21	Iowa	Miner	" " "
Brown, John William	41	New York	"	Greenwood Valley.
Bayley, Alexander John	38	Vermont	Farmer	Pilot Hill.
Bishop, John	45	Maryland	Miner	"
Buckner, T. Merriweath'r	46	Kentucky	"	Greenwood Valley.
Bell, Alexander Gibson	31	New York	"	Spanish Dry Diggings.
Brown, William Henry	34	New Jersey	"	" " "
Burner, Geo. Washington	21	Ohio	"	" " "
Brown, Major Daniel	52	Pennsylvania	"	Pilot Hill.
Boswell, Alex'r Jackson	41	Tennessee	"	"
Baker, Joshua	34	New York	Saloon Keeper	Shingle Springs.
Bird, Albert Brigham	42	Kentucky	Butcher	Latrobe.
Bowker, Milo Anderson	44	Vermont	Laborer	El Dorado.
Barber, Thomas Allen	39	Connecticut	Physician	Latrobe.
Bennett, Damascus	35	Missouri	Miner	Near El Dorado.
Bennett, William	21	Illinois	Laborer	Duroc.
Brown, James Garland	41	Alabama	"	Shingle Springs.
Bailey, James Green	38	Virginia	Dep. Constable	" "
Bayless, William	38	Tennesse	Physician	El Dorado.
Bitzer, Urias	40	Pennsylvania	Miner	Near Latrobe.

NAMES.	Age	Place of Nativity.	Occupation.	Local Residence.
Burlingham, Nat'n Dec'tr	34	New York	Miner	Logtown.
Bown, Geo. Washington	34	Pennsylvania	"	Near El Dorado.
Bown, Abraham	52	Pennsylvania	"	" "
Buckner, John Wash'ton.	33	Missouri	"	Duncan's Store.
Bentley, Geo. Washing'tn	41	Kentucky	Saloon Keeper	Shingle Springs.
Bunis, James	50	Kentucky	Miner	" "
Bennett, Joseph William	34	Missouri	"	El Dorado.
Bryant, Jas. Mereweather.	49	Kentucky	"	
Babcox, Jefferson T.	45	New York	Engineer	Aurum City.
Berrisford, Alfred	37	Great Britain	Miner	Greenwood Township.
Baker, Benjamin	36	Russia	Clerk	Mud Springs.
Borneman, Louis	41	Germany	Saloon Keeper	Kelsey.
Burk, William	29	Canada	Water Agent	"
Brentz, William Hurley	46	Kentucky	Miner	Placerville.
Bailey, James	40	Ireland	"	"
Bannon, Patrick	55	Ireland	Merchant	White Oak.
Burk, James	30	Canada	Miner	Kelsey.
Bunce, Daniel	50	England	Farmer	Greenwood.
Banholzer, Antone	49	Germany	"	Clarksville.
Bates, Zealous	35	Massachusetts	Collector	"
Brown, James	32	West Virginia	Miner	Placerville.
Brindupky, Frederick	35	Prussia	Farmer	Shingle Springs.
Bittinger, George Jacob	51	Bavaria	"	Diamond Springs.
Baxter, Thomas	45	Ireland	Miner	Shingle Springs.
Brandon, Andrew	31	Illinois	"	White Oak.
Bechere, Franz	39	Germany	"	Grizzly Flat.
Bruce, George	52	Scotland	"	Placerville.
Bryant, Alexander	37	New York	Lumberman	" Pacific H.
Breese, David	38	Canada	Miner	Mud Springs.
Bachelor, John	36	Prussia	"	Fair Play, Cosumnes.
Borgwardt, Henry	34	Germany	"	Kelsey Township.
Beaman, Theodore	36	New York	"	Georgetown.
Borland, Alexander	49	Scotland	Shoemaker	"
Black, Samuel	62	Maine	Miner	"
Baldwin, J. Washington	42	Pennsylvania	"	"
Buck, Lewis	40	Hamburg	"	"
Barklage, Gerdard	39	Hanover	Merchant	"
Berry, Solomon Adams	60	Maine	Hotel Keeper	"
Bryson, George Charles	43	Scotland	Miner	"
Brown, George	44	England	"	"
Bachi, William	36	Switzerland	Bar Keeper	"
Beattie, George	40	Scotland	Miner	"
Boyle, John	43	Ireland	"	"
Besslin, Jacob	37	Wirtemburg	"	Greenwood Valley.
Brown, Charles	54	Great Britain	"	Salmon Falls.
Braderick, Isaac	33	Ohio	Ditch Agent	" "
Boarman, Michael	34	Bavaria	Miner	Greenwood Township.
Bramer, Frederick	34	Holland	"	Coloma.
Beswich, James	64	England	"	Newtown.
Brown, John Love	38	Tennessee	"	White Oak Township.
Benniger, Conrad	45	Switzerland	"	Salmon Falls Township.
Balken, Jacob	41	Prussia	Farmer	" " "
Barr, Benjamin Franklin	45	Maryland	Carpenter	" " "
Bounn, Henry	43	Hanover	Farmer	White Oak "
Bremer, John Frederick	45	Denmark	Lawyer	" " "
Broadbent Stephen	57	England	Miner	Mud Springs "
Borger, George	51	Baden	Tailor	" " "
Burston, William	42	England	Brewer	" " "
Barrette, Guilliam	44	Canada	Farmer	" " "
Brosseau, Louis	36	Great Britain	Miner	" " "
Bissell, Gustavus	36	Massachusetts	Farmer	White Oak "
Brindupky, Charles	33	Prussia	"	Mud Springs "
Briggs, Fordyce Wiswall	30	Massachusetts	Clerk	" " "

NAME.	Age	Place of Nativity.	Occupation.	Local Residence.
Becherrer, Jacob	43	Baden	Farmer	Mountain Township.
Bartlette, James	47	Great Britain	"	" "
Brockmire, Henry	41	Prussia	Miner	Cosumnes "
Buechler, John	45	France	"	Georgetown "
Burmann, Heinreich	45	Denmark	Carpenter	Coloma "
Barrett, Josiah	35	Great Britain	Farmer	White Oak "
Barth, Christian	40	Bavaria	Miner	" " "
Bey, Henry	57	Hanover	"	Coloma "
Brown, Francis Marion	28	Virginia	"	Placerville "
Baker, Henry	47	Germany	Farmer	Diamond Springs T'p.
Baldy, John	32	Pennsylvania	Miner	" " "
Berryhill, John Rutlidge	48	Georgia	"	Placerville "
Bailey, Nelson	45	Pennsylvania	"	" "
Blair, Edwin	36	Missouri	Stage Driver	Lake Valley "
Brown, Jesse	37	New York	Butcher	Placerville, Dicks. R.
Barklage, William	26	Hanover	Clerk	Georgetown.
Belitz, Julius	42	Prussia	Farmer	Placerville Township.
Belitz, Charles	39	France	"	" "
Burns, Thomas Z.	42	Pennsylvania	Mail Agent	Diamond Springs T'p.
Bennett, William Henry	24	England	Miner	Salmon Falls "
Bradenchel, Leon	34	France	"	Diamond Springs "
Brown, Jacob	41	Ohio	Laborer	Mud Springs "
Bunker, Charles Albert	25	Maine	Mechanic	Grizzly Flat.
Baird, Jefferson	40	Pennsylvania	Sawyer	" "
Baumgardner, Anthony	29	Ohio	Carpenter	Placerville.
Behrns, George	38	Denmark	Farmer	Kelsey Township.
Brandeman, John	42	Denmark	Miner	Greenwood.
Blair, James	37	Scotland	Hotel keeper	Placerville Township.
Bosworth, Charles	36	England	Miner	" "
Beckman, Henry	42	Prussia	"	Coloma "
Boyle, William	30	Great Britain	"	Placerville "
Broekman, Jacob Frio	43	Germany	Farmer	Gold Hill.
Biogiotti, Luiji	27	Italy	Miner	Placerville Township.
Brown, John	48	Germany	Stone mason	Coloma "
Brink, William Bickney	56	Pennsylvania	Physician	Georgetown.
Brashaer, Cuthburt Sid	56	Kentucky	Miner	Volcanoville.
Bitters, Jonas	37	Pennsylvania	"	Mt. Gregory.
Boswell, Rufus Frisley	27	Tennessee	Teamster	Diamond Springs.
Bryon, Napoleon B.	36	Indiana	Farmer	Sly Park.
Bryant, Herman Leroy	26	New York	Laborer	" "
Brewer, William Hibbard	32	Ohio	Miner	Diamond Springs.
Beard, Miligan	30	Indiana	Teamster	" "
Breeze, Thomas William	37	Virginia	Farmer	Coloma Township.
Barnes, Richard Edward	45	Connecticut	Miner	Gold Hill.
Bellion, George Andrew	39	Kentucky	"	" "
Broton, Shebrich Hobart	68	Vermont	Farmer	Coloma.
Buell, Rufus	64	Massachusetts	"	Cold Springs.
Bradberry, Mathew	33	Tennessee	"	El Dorado.
Barr, John Robert	27	Pennsylvania	Miner	Shingle Springs.
Burgess, Thomas Warfield	41	Maryland	Merchant	El Dorado.
Butler, John Marmaduke	39	Vermont	Miner	" "
Bagley, Richard Archb'ld	45	Virginia	"	" "
Bryant, Edward Spencer	42	New York	Farmer	Latrobe.
Best, James David	34	Kentucky	Laborer	"
Beal, William Careal	38	Tennessee	"	"
Brandon, Zar Price	46	Ohio	Farmer	"
Hiers, John	35	Ohio	Blacksmith	"
Barryman, Robert Allen	29	Ohio	Miner	Shingle Springs.
Ballance, Silas	33	Kentucky	"	Nashville.
Brown, Absalom	40	Missouri	"	"
Barnes, William Albert	34	Tennessee	"	El Dorado.
Babcox, Jefferson T.	46	New York	Engineer	" "
Bailey, Robert	31	Ohio	Miner	Coyoteville.

NAME.	Age	Place of Nativity.	Occupation.	Local Residence.
Busan, Andrew McCauley	34	Illinois	Musician	Fair Play.
Bonham, John	25	Ohio	Miner	Brownsville.
Barton, Timothy Guy	37	New York	Farmer	White Oak Township.
Bantz, Addison Sylvester.	32	Pennsylvania	Miner	" " "
Burkhardt, Peter	31	Pennsylvania	Laborer	Placerville "
Bradford, Caleb	44	Vermont	Miner	Kelsey "
Bertch, Joshua	33	Pennsylvania	"	"
Boswell, Andrew Jackson	41	Tennessee	"	Pilot Hill.
Brown, Gilbert Nourse	24	Maine	"	"
Blackmer, Elbert Scran...	40	New York	"	"
Blue, Samuel Stout	40	New York	"	"
Bemis, Samuel Cooper	50	N. Hampshire.	Shingle-maker.	Placerville Township.
Brownell, James	51	Massachusetts	Farmer	" "
Brownell, Jere. Devoll	31	Massachusetts	"	" "
Bemas, Eugene Madison..	31	Ohio	Lawyer	" "
Branthover, Adam	36	Pennsylvania	Miner	Grizzly Flat.
Bunker, Charles Albert	25	Maine	Machinist	" "
Bahnson, Herman	48	Germany	Farmer	Gold Hill.
Barlow, Alexander	33	Kentucky	Miner	"
Bascom, Franklin	48	Vermont	Hotel-keeper	Smith's Flat.
Barkla, John Samuel	35	England	Miner	Diamond Springs.
Black, Isaac Snow	41	Maine	Carpenter	Georgetown.
Barker, Charles	54	N. Hampshire.	Miner	"
Barker, Madison Cleave.	31	Georgia	"	"
Breedlove, James Warren.	39	Tennessee	Laborer	"
Bowman, Israel	24	Ohio	Farmer	" Township.
Bowker, John	51	New York	"	"
Bryant, Nathaniel	43	Massachusetts	Miner	"
Bowman, Elisha James	46	New York	Hotel-keeper	Placerville Township.
Beaver, Lewis Timmons	30	Illinois	Laborer	"
Bartram, Porter	28	Ohio	"	"
Boyer, George Washingt'n	37	Illinois	"	"
Babe, Jerome Lewellyn	30	Missouri	Miner	"
Bidstrut, Hans William	31	Denmark	Farmer	Mud Springs.
Bryant, Anson Brown	35	Ohio	Dairyman	Dick's Ranch.
Brooks, Chas. Shadrach	35	New York	Miner	Mud Springs T'p.
Barnet, Houseman	68	New York	"	Salmon Falls.
Boero, Dominico	34	Italy	Cook	Placerville.
Bolluff, Joseph	24	Germany	Wood-chopper..	Georgetown.
Beatty, John Crawford	23	Ireland	Miner	"
Brewster, George Wash	27	New York	Clerk	Placerville.
Bouton, Andrew Pettis	47	New York	Miner	Georgetown.
Bennett, William Francis.	21	Illinois	"	"
Beebe, Oliver Cleveland	38	New York	"	"
Bradford, George Lewis.	36	Massachusetts	"	"
Bigelow, William	42	Connecticut	Farmer	Georgetown Township
Bean, Samuel	28	N. Hampshire.	Laborer	Lake Valley "
Bennett, Elnathan	39	New York	Hotel-keeper.	" " "
Brown, David Provost	40	New Jersey	Miner	Pilot Hill.
Burpee, Dwight	45	Massachusetts	"	" "
Burns, Thomas	33	Maine	"	Grizzly Flat.
Bullard, John Warren	44	Ohio	Farmer	" "
Bailey, Seth	38	Missouri	Miner	Indian Diggings.
Burrows, Josiah	31	Ohio	Mason	Latrobe.
Baldy, Edward	35	Pennsylvania	Laborer	El Dorado.
Burgoon, John C	44	Pennsylvania	Miner	King's Store.
Burgoon, Jacob	39	Pennsylvania	"	" "
Burks, Charles	51	Kentucky	"	Shingle Springs.
Bishop, William Spencer.	32	New York	Saloon-keeper	" "
Brown, Levi	62	New York	Farmer	Latrobe.
Buffington, James Riley	30	Illinois	"	"
Brown, William W	37	Pennsylvania	Miner	Mud Springs.
Busick, John Monroe	32	Kentucky	Hotel-keeper	" "

NAMES.	Age	Place of Nativity.	Occupation.	Local Residence.
Bolander, John	36	Ohio	Laborer	Mud Springs.
Beedle, Hiram	45	Ohio	Farmer	El Dorado.
Bernardi, Felice	28	Switzerland	Miner	Newtown.
Berry, Irad Fuller	39	New York	Laborer	Strawberry Valley.
Burrell, Martin	29	New York	Teamster	Placerville Township.
Blanchard, William Wert.	31	Vermont	"	" "
Bragg, Albert	51	Maine	Carriage Maker.	Grizzly Flat.
Breedlove, James Milton	32	Virginia	Teamster	Travers Creek.

C

NAMES.	Age	Place of Nativity.	Occupation.	Local Residence.
Carlin, James	37	Ireland	Clerk	Uniontown.
Crain, Sylvester Kelley	34	N. Hampshire.	Miner	Clarksville.
Cummins, David	45	Pennsylvania.	Postmaster	"
Curtis, Thomas	43	Tennessee	Miner	White Oak Township.
Conklin, Charles	29	New York	"	Clarksville.
Chesim, William	40	Ohio	Farmer	"
Christison, John	52	Kentucky	"	"
Chase, James Franklin	40	Massachusetts	Miner	White Oak Township.
Calyer, Peter	37	New York	Farmer	" "
Cook, William Cookman	71	England	Miner	Placerville "
Christie, Andrew Jackson	42	New York	Farmer	Gold Hill.
Cooper, William Horton	65	England	Justice Peace	Placerville.
Center, Samuel Henry	38	N. Hampshire.	Ranchman	Mud Springs Township.
Carrigan, John	60	Ireland	Miner	Clarksville.
Chick, Geo. Washington	37	Virginia	Mason	Placerville.
Coleman, Asa	55	Massachusetts	Clerk	"
Crawford, Fred. Gustavus	34	New York	Farmer	White Oak Township.
Celio, Charles Joseph	33	Switzerland	Milkman	Placerville.
Coyle, Francis	36	Ireland	Miner	White Oak Township.
Cottrell, Andrew Jackson	40	Ohio	Teamster	Placerville.
Carpenter, Gideon Judd	42	Pennsylvania.	Lawyer	"
Conklin, Edward Barber	44	New York	Teacher	"
Child, Stanley Faber	47	New York	Druggist	Coloma.
Cutting, Hiram Edward	46	Vermont	Miner	Placerville.
Craddock, John	44	Great Britain	Farmer	"
Cummings, Leander	39	Vermont	Teacher	Cosumnes Township.
Carney, John	38	New York	Clerk	Shingle Springs.
Curless, Biar	33	Indiana	Miner	Smith's Flat.
Crosley, William	56		Farmer	"
Clees, John Peter	32	Holland	Saloon Keeper	Placerville.
Costallo, Michael	43	Great Britain	Miner	Coloma.
Connor, William	37	Ireland	"	"
Coats, Benjamin	67	Pennsylvania.	"	Placerville Township.
Clark, Caiaphas	59	England	Shoemaker	"
Cooley, Samuel Burr	38	Connecticut	Laundryman	"
Christian, Francis	63	Canada	Miller	" Township.
Chalmers, Robert	46	Great Britain	Collector	Coloma.
Clark, Joshua	21	Indiana	Butcher	"
Cartheche, John	44	Greece	Jailor	Placerville.
Casteel, Pierce	39	Ohio	Speculator	"
Cook, John	38	Maryland	Physician	"
Clifton, Richard	52	England	Miner	" Township.
Crisman, Chas. Lafayette	49	Pennsylvania.	Carpenter	"
Creighton, James	43	Maine	Miner	Smith's Flat.
Clement, Joseph	62	New York	Moulder	Placerville.
Christian, Jonas	37	New York	Machinist	"
Christian, Edwin	30	Illinois	Blacksmith	"
Collins, Frederick	35	Massachusetts	Clerk	"
Callen, Christopher	35	Ireland	Laborer	"
Cruson, Thomas	63	Kentucky	Miner	Reservoir Hill.
Coffin, Oliver	30	Indiana	"	Placerville.
Collins, Henry Merchant	34	New York	Clerk	"
Carpenter, William Pitt	35	Vermont	Miner	Smith's Flat.

NAME.	Age	Place of Nativity.	Occupation.	Local Residence.
Crosley, John Sellers	32	Ohio	Miner	Smith's Flat.
Crowder, Jere. Jackson	33	North Carolina	Stage Driver	Placerville.
Cook, John Wesley	28	Ohio	Miner	Smith's Flat.
Crocker, Benj. Stoddard	39	Virginia	Farmer	Placerville.
Coville, Benj. Hows	34	Massachusetts	Miner	"
Calloway, Wm. Thomas	43	New York	Shoemaker	"
Clayton, Marion Francis	39	Ohio	Physician	"
Chichester, Daniel Wood	34	New York	Lumber M'rch't	"
Clark, David	36	Ohio	Miner	" Township.
Convis, Wm. Wallace	26	Michigan	Teamster	"
Crippen, John	65	Delaware	Wood-chopper	" Township.
Cassidy, Samuel	34	Ireland	Laborer	Shingle Springs.
Carberry, Michael	48	Ireland	Gardner	Placerville.
Covington, J. Stoughton	46	Virginia	Miner	"
Corson, Moses Sylvester	31	Maine	Harness-maker	"
Campini, Anselmo	25	Switzerland	Dairyman	"
Culver, Edwin Sherer	24	New York	Printer	"
Claypoole, Mathew	33	Ohio	Laborer	" Township.
Coats, Wm. James	38	Indiana	Miner	Smith's Flat.
Carter, Job Lindsey	39	Tennessee	"	" "
Crocker, Wm. Henry	34	Missouri	Farmer	Placerville.
Caldwell, Adam	51	Great Britain	Miner	Loafers' Hollow.
Clifton, John Griffith	26	Wisconsin	"	Placerville Township.
Cocksbill, James	40	England	"	Gold Hill.
Colver, Richard Pelton	59	New York	Millwright	Placerville.
Childs, Charles Wesley	23	New York	School Teacher	Smith's Flat.
Cole, Wm. Bowen	59	Massachusetts	Laborer	Placerville Township.
Curecco, Stefano	41	Switzerland	Milkman	" "
Cronart, Charles Henry	23	New York	Butcher	"
Campbell, Jas. Solomon	44	New York	Merchant	Salmon Falls.
Capuro, John	25	Italy	Miner	Diamond Springs.
Clydesdale, John	39	Ireland	"	Negro Hill, Sal. Falls.
Crocker, John	42	Maryland	Farmer	Coloma.
Corliss, Joseph Haynes	44	New Jersey	"	Uniontown.
Clark, Robert Valentine	47	Indiana	Butcher	Coloma.
Clark, Wm. Goldson	25	Indiana	"	"
Cappleman, John Wm	24	Alabama	Farmer	Uniontown.
Congdon, Geo. Champlin	50	New York	Hotel-keeper	Placerville.
Church, Wm. Wadsworth	35	Ohio	Baker	"
Channel, John Hamilton	32	N. Hampshire	Miner	"
Chamblin, Israel T. G.	40	Virginia	Lumberman	Sportsman's Hall.
Colborn, Saml. Densmore	48	Vermont	Farmer	Kelsey.
Craig, John	42	Ireland	Miner	Clarksville.
Cornur, Simeon Tivis	37	Missouri	"	Diamond Springs.
Crane, Edward Ames	44	New Jersey	"	" "
Chipman, N. Atwood, jr.	27	Massachusetts	"	" Township.
Caldwell, Crawford	47	Ohio	Physician	" "
Carpenter, Caleb Gardner	49	New York	Farmer	" "
Chapman, Joseph	31	Indiana	Miner	" "
Camp, Asa Stevens	37	Pennsylvania	Laborer	Kelsey "
Carra, John	32	England	Merchant	White Oak "
Chalmers, George	28	Great Britain	"	Placerville.
Christian, William	47	Great Britain	Farmer	Grizzly Flat.
Cobb, John Ransom	37	New York	"	Kelsey Township.
Crooks, Michael	68	Ireland	Miner	" "
Clark, Thomas	38	Ireland	Miner	Coloma.
Crippen, Jonas Jackson	37	Ohio	Teamster	Placerville.
Collins, William	58	Indiana	Miner	Georgetown.
Crawford, Ellison Lassell	34	Maine	Attorn'y at Law	"
Carrothers, James	54	Pennsylvania	Miner	"
Cooper, John	44	Vermont	"	"
Collins, Lewis	60	Kentucky	Farmer	"
Crumpton, Jno. Wheeler	23	Missouri	Miner	"

NAME.	Age	Place of Nativity.	Occupation.	Local Residence.
Chapman, Andrew	46	S. Carolina	Teamster	Alabama Flat.
Cushman, Robert	38	Massachusetts	Miner	Georgetown.
Clark, Geo. Washington	49	Kentucky	Clerk	Garden Valley.
Clinton, Alexander, sr	66	Maryland	Carpenter	" "
Clinton, Alexander, jr	35	New York	"	" "
Cook, William Newton	32	Indiana	Miner	Travers' Creek.
Clifford, David Agnew	30	Pennsylvania	Cook	Strawberry Valley.
Campbell, Amaziah Frank	28	Pennsylvania	Laborer	Lake Valley.
Clement, Ephraim	53	N. Hampshire	Hotel-keeper	" "
Crawford, William Hay	37	Pennsylvania	Miner	Coloma.
Corliss, Charles Pulaski	28	New York	Farmer	Uniontown.
Crocker, James	33	Ohio	"	Coloma.
Croft, Droft	35	Ohio	Miner	Kelsey Township.
Coe, William	63	Ohio	Farmer	" "
Coe, William Franklin	26	Indiana	"	" "
Coe, John Milton	24	Indiana	"	" "
Coe, Francis Marion	28	Indiana	"	" "
Carrothers, Walter	45	Ohio	"	" "
Chase, John William	37	Massachusetts	"	" "
Curtis, Charles Burke	35	Connecticut	Miner	" "
Card, Alexander	32	New York	Lumberman	Diamond Springs.
Cutler, Luth. Chamberlin	48	Maine	Farmer	" "
Claibourne, Robert King	35	Tennessee	"	Indian Diggings.
Cable, John	41	Tennessee	Saloon-keeper	" "
Cameron, Thomas	54	Maryland	Hotel-keeper	" "
Copper, Wm. Alexander	50	Maryland	Farmer	" "
Colby, Henry Monroe	27	Maine	Laborer	" "
Crabtree, Francis Asbery	40	Virginia	Miner	Fair Play.
Claybrook, Malcer Ferris	31	Missouri	"	" "
Carr, Joseph Gorham	33	Maine	Store-keeper	" "
Church, Alonzo	40	New York	"	Perry's Creek.
Claghorn, Geo. Spaulding	43	Georgia	Miner	Fair Play.
Chote, John Brown	42	Alabama	Farmer	Middle Fork, Cos. R.
Curtis, Luther Bates	46	New York	Miner	Greenwood.
Calderwood, Geo. Judson	29	Maine	"	Pilot Hill.
Clark, David Ditch	30	Illinois	"	" "
Creque, William Konover	55	New Jersey	Hotel-keeper	" "
Coffin, Nathaniel Macy	63	New York	Miner	Greenwood.
Crane, Samuel Scott	61	Kentucky	"	" "
Crane, Charles Henry	24	Kentucky	"	" "
Clow, Stephen Carlton	38	Vermont	Blacksmith	Pilot Hill.
Clark, William Henry	36	New York	Farmer	Shingle Springs.
Coddington, Geo. Wash	42	Ohio	Cash.P.&S.V.R.	" "
Cooley, Charles	31	Massachusetts	Saloon-keeper	" "
Camp, James Monroe	31	Michigan	Merchant	" "
Cotton, William Fletcher	38	New York	Ditch Agent	El Dorado.
Close, Seymour	66	New York	Farmer	Logtown.
Caughey, Wm. Whiteside	39	Pennsylvania	Miner	Latrobe.
Chambers, David Coons	43	Kentucky	"	El Dorado.
Cooley, Jerome Bonaparte	43	Tennessee	"	Georgetown Township
Chipman, Isaiah Mayo	39	Massachusetts	Farmer	Mud Springs.
Crooks, George	41	Scotland	Carpenter	Salmon Falls.
Cook, William Smith	39	Georgia	Miner	Latrobe.
Chapman, John	39	Georgia	Farmer	Georgetown Township
Cummings, Milton Robins	57	Maine	Laborer	Gold Hill.
Carpenter, Nicholous	61	Ohio	Farmer	Kelsey Township.
Cary, David Ward	58	New York	Miner	Georgetown.
Carporo, Joseph	30	Italy	"	Newtown.
Crain, Levant	40	New York	"	Georgetown.
Coppinger, Thomas	42	Ireland	Bar-keeper	"
Cutter, Thomas Jefferson	41	Maine	Miner	"
Cowley, George	39	England	"	"
Clark, Henry Houston	21	Michigan	"	"

NAMES.	Age	Place of Nativity.	Occupation.	Local Residence.
Collins, Jeremiah	32	Tennessee	Miner	Georgetown.
Copley, Andrew Jackson	36	New York	"	"
Cox, Rodger	44	Great Britain	"	Coloma.
Claasen, Paul Pay	23	Great Britain	"	"
Cole, Louis	54	Virginia	"	White Oak.
Calloway, Patrick Henry	38	Missouri	Blacksmith	" "
Cline, Henry	36	New York	Engineer	Salmon Falls.
Cooley, Chauncey	29	Illinois	Shoemaker	Mud Springs.
Crandall, Cyren's Black'r	42	New York	Blacksmith	" "
Cline, David Ambrose	35	Missouri	Miner	" "
Curran, John	41	Ireland	"	" "
Carroll, Patrick	37	Ireland	Laborer	" "
Carson, Daniel Robert	38	England	Bridge keeper	Mountain Township.
Cowl, William Henry	41	Great Britain	Miner	" "
Clark, Joshua	22	Massachusetts	Laborer	" "
Christian, William Briden	23	Great Britain	Miner	" "
Crowly, John	55	Great Britain	"	Cosumnes "
Chouleur, Martin	59	France	"	Diamond Springs.
Clifford, Michael	40	Ireland	"	White Oak.
Chouleur, John	57	France	"	Diamond Springs.
Comins, Cooper	41	England	Blacksmith	Mud Springs.
Cole, Hiram Seely	38	New York	Teamster	Lake Valley.
Collins, Fitz Jackson	48	New York	Miner	Georgetown.
Craven, Joseph	47	England	"	Mud Springs.
Christian, Henry	41	New York	Machinist	Placerville.
Coan, Thompson John	28	Vermont	Miner	White Oak Township.
Cooper, Stephen	47	England	"	Diamond Springs.
Cato, William	35	Switzerland	Farmer	" "
Carlton, Charles Henry	32	N. Hampshire	Miner	Smith Flat.
Clark, Joseph " E. W."	38	New York	"	Placerville.
Coom, Joseph	45	England	"	" Township.
Crippen, John J	30	Ohio	Laborer	"
Clark, Jaazaniah Richard	48	Massachusetts	Miner	Salmon Falls Township
Curran, James	34	Ireland	"	Diamond Springs.
Cohn, Edward	36	Prussia	Tailor	Placerville.
Childs, William Wallace	49	New York	Farmer	" Township.
Chapman, Barney	47	North Carolina	Miner	Coloma.
Cowin, William	41	Scotland	Toll Collector	Smith's Flat.
Cass, Andrew	32	Ireland	Miner	Gold Hill.
Charles, Andrew	27	Greece	"	Placerville.
Campini, Vincent	32	Switzerland	Dairyman	"
Campini, Luiji	23	Switzerland	"	"
Collins, John Wesley	27	Mississippi	Farmer	Georgetown.
Craig, Daniel Boon	49	Missouri	Ditch Agent	"
Coob, Theophalus	51	Virginia	Miner	Volcanoville.
Corwin, John Glasbie	39	Ohio	"	Georgetown.
Carpenter, Jesse	67	Pennsylvania	"	Volcanoville.
Collins, William Hohman	21	Illinois	"	Georgetown.
Calmes, Charles Henry	48	Kentucky	Ditch Agent	"
Choroning, Marq. Lafay'te	53	Tennessee	Miner	"
Cunningham, William	46	Virginia	Farmer	Pleasant Valley.
Chapman, Caleb Peacock	47	Indiana	Druggist	Diamond Springs
Crowell, Walter	38	New York	Farmer	Gold Hill.
Canfield, Joseph Gils	45	New York	Merchant	Coloma.
Covey, Benjamin	49	Virginia	Miner	Gold Hill.
Cromwell, William Oscar	29	Maryland	"	Uniontown.
Cromwell, William	58	Maryland	"	"
Carney, Smith	40	New Jersey	Farmer	"
Cryst, Wesley	37	Virginia	Miner	El Dorado.
Calar, Jacob	46	Tennessee	"	"
Chanler, Evin Russell	34	North Carolina	"	Nashville.
Chaffin, Geo. Washington	38	Ohio	Teamster	Shingle Springs.
Conn, John	37	Illinois	Miner	El Dorado.

NAME.	Age	Place of Nativity.	Occupation.	Local Residence.
Chilton, Anselen Lynch	43	Virginia	Rancher	Nashville.
Cantrill, John	39	New York	Miner	Cosumnes Township.
Carck, James Thomas	27	Massachusetts	Stonecutter	" "
Chadburn, Emry	33	Maine	Miner	White Oak "
Church, Alva William	31	New York	Engineer	" "
Crawford, Myron	49	New York	Teamster	" "
Chase, Warren	34	N. Hampshire	Miner	" "
Cochenour, William	40	Pennsylvania	"	Kelsey Township.
Carpenter, S. Mannoah	27	Iowa	"	"
Carpenter, N. Armstrong	34	Indiana	"	"
Cook, Benjamin Franklin	39	Indiana	"	"
Carpenter, John Sales	36	Indiana	"	"
Clark, James	40	New York	"	Pilot Hill.
Cason, James	69	Virginia	Laborer	Salmon Falls.
Coffin, Oliver	31	Indiana	Miner	Placerville.
Clifton, William	21	Illinois	Teamster	"
Coats, George Franklin	32	Illinois	Miner	Smith's Flat.
Cody, Patrick Henry	39	New York	Farmer	Placerville.
Crooks, David	32	New Jersey	Miner	Grizzly Flat.
Claassen, Nummel Sturdt	26	Great Britain	"	White Oak Township.
Claassen, Peter Hanson	28	Great Britain	"	" " "
Clemmonson, John	39	Denmark	"	Placerville.
Carlock, Jacob	33	Ohio	Teamster	Georgetown.
Clark, Francis Henry	34	Pennsylvania	Miner	"
Collins, William Clayton	34	Mississippi	Farmer	"
Cleaves, James Ross	31	Maine	Jeweler	"
Casey, James Fraser	36	Tennessee	Miner	Sly Park.
Coffin, Hudson Waldon	33	New York	"	Pleasant Valley.
Clow, Francis	62	New York	Laborer	Diamond Springs.
Conner, John	47	Indiana	Miner	Pleasant Valley.
Cox, Henry Samuel	26	Tennessee	"	"
Courtois, Charles	33	Missouri	Engineer	Sly Park
Chappell, Richard	31	Pennsylvania	Carpenter	"
Cummins, Jas. Anderson	35	New York	Miner	Pleasant Valley.
Cox, William Harrison	27	Indiana	"	Placerville.
Crippen, Charles	44	Ohio	Teamster	"
Carlson, John	27	Sweden	Miner	Diamond Springs.
Conklin, Charles	30	New York	"	White Oak.
Caystile, Thomas	56	England	Butcher	Placerville.
Carey, John	40	Ireland	Miner	Georgetown.
Current, Hugh Sheren	26	Canada	"	"
Craddock, Richard	21	England	"	Placerville.
Cleekler, Edward	38	Germany	Carpenter	"
Cooley, Irvin	35	Missouri	Miner	White Oak.
Collins, Geo. Washington	40	Maryland	"	Georgetown.
Carter, Edward	54	Massachusetts	Minister	"
Crawford, James	34	Vermont	Carpenter	Salmon Falls.
Carpenter, William	36	New York	Blacksmith	" "
Castor, Joseph Edward	45	Pennsylvania	Miner	" "
Chandler, Josiah Henry	31	New York	Farmer	Cold Springs.
Case, Lafayette Wash'ton	33	Massachusetts	Laborer	Placerville.
Cope, Benjamin Martin	32	Pennsylvania	Miner	Cosumnes Township.
Caldwell, John Alexander	42	Pennsylvania	"	Mud Springs.
Coleman, Henry Martin	33	Pennsylvania	"	Shingle Springs.
Comos, Thomas	32	Kentucky	Laborer	"
Chancy, David Cyrus	27	Ohio	Farmer	Latrobe.
Chawvin, Augustus "C"	43	Missouri	Merchant	King's Store.
Crawford, And. Jackson	34	Tennessee	Laborer	Latrobe.
Crist, Henry Holstone	40	Virginia	Painter	"
Cleveland, Joseph	54	Canada	Shingle-maker	Sportsman Hall.
Crues, Jose	27	Switzerland	Miner	Georgetown.
Chalmers, Alexander	25	Great Britain	Merchant	Coloma.
Croy, Morgan Jonathan	33	Ohio	Teamster	Placerville Township.

NAME.	Age	Place of Nativity.	Occupation.	Local Residence.
Chapel, Benj. Andrew	35	New York	Landlord	Placerville Township.

D

NAME.	Age	Place of Nativity.	Occupation.	Local Residence.
Duden, George	55	Pennsylvania	Dep. Recorder	Placerville.
Davis, Charles	44	Massachusetts	Miner	Jay Hawk.
Donohoe, Wm. Meagher	36	Ireland	Liquor Merch't	Placerville.
De Golia, Darwin	48	New York	Farmer	"
Dreyer, George Frank	30	Hamburg	Saloon-keeper	"
Davey, Wm. Henry	26	England	Teamster	" Township.
Davis, Wm. George	61	Virginia	Miner	"
Davis, Lewis Marvis	39	Maine	Farmer	Mud Springs.
Dormady, William	69	Ireland	"	White Oak Township.
Davis, Luther	48	Massachusetts	Merchant	Coloma.
Dailey, James	38	Ireland	Carpenter	Diamond Springs.
Dunlap, Elon	36	New York	Toll-keeper	Mud Springs.
Dascomb, C. E. Augustus	23	Massachusetts	Teacher	Placerville.
Dempsey, Peter	40	Ireland	Laborer	"
Danz Paul	38	Switzerland	Dairyman	"
Duffin, James	68	Ireland	Miner	Coloma.
Duffin, John	34	Canada	"	"
Daly, Patrick	40	Ireland	"	Placerville Township.
Dracksall, John	51	Bavaria	Gardner	Newtown.
Dilley, Josiah Vandiver	36	Indiana	Miner	Placerville.
Douglass, Jos. McCuen	46	Kentucky	Broker	"
Dunn, Maurice	33	Ireland	Blacksmith	"
Dunn, Daniel	27	Ireland	Blacksmith	"
Dunker, Herman	39	Hanover	Blacksmith	White Oak Township.
Dickey, John Truman	44	Pennsylvania	Farmer	Mud Springs.
Darlington, Abraham	45	New Jersey	Merchant	Placerville Township.
Desalme, Edward	32	Missouri	Blacksmith	" "
De Witt, Saml. Bradley	31	Ohio	Miner	" "
Dalton, John	48	Pennsylvania	Farmer	" "
Dimon, John	39	New York	Miner	" "
Davis, Seneca	32	Vermont	"	" "
Davis, Daniel	62	Maine	Wagon-maker	" "
Dascomb, Thos. Ransford	72	Massachusetts	Miner	" "
Davis, Ewd. Livingston	33	North Carolina	Store-keeper	" "
Dean, Joseph Miller	43	Ohio	Sawyer	"
Dugan, Wm	43	Ireland	Farmer	Mud Springs.
Daingerfield, Edwin B	38	Virginia	"	Pacerville Township.
Donaldson, John	37	Scotland	Miner	Smith's Flat.
Dupan, John	32	New York	Stewart	Placerville.
Desalme, John	39	France	Blacksmith	Smith's Flat.
Desalme, Joseph	42	France	Miner	" "
Day, Ephraim Cooper	59	Ohio	Farmer	Kelsey Township.
Dingman, Henry Lorenzo	44	New York	"	Placerville Township.
Davis, Wm	36	Great Britain	Miner	"
Demuth, Reuben	40	Pennsylvania	Lumberman	Kelsey.
Dunn, Thomas	54	Ireland	Blacksmith	Placerville.
Duncan, George Edward	55	Massachusetts	Farmer	Sly Park.
De Wolfe, Jos. Brown	37	Maine	Miner	Mud Springs.
Davis, Wm. Thomas	31	Vermont	"	Coloma.
Dobson, Joseph	28	Illinois	Farmer	Gold Hill.
Day, Henry	66	Massachusetts	Saddler	Coloma.
Draper, Emerson Henry	33	Massachusetts	Farmer	Clarksville.
Davison, T. W. Greenleaf	61	Massachusetts	Miner	Kelsey Creek.
Dubrey, Louis	37	Missouri	Farmer	Indian Diggings.
Dench, John Wm	38	Ohio	Harness-maker	Placerville.
Drinkerhoff, Fred. Martin	34	Maryland	Miner	"
Dickson, J. W. Bushnell	37	Pennsylvania	Farmer	"
Dennis, Mathew "Q"	38	Kentucky	Barkeeper	" Township.
Day, Wm. Spear	48	New York	Merchant	Diamond Springs.
Dean, Isaac Jerry	27	New York	Blacksmith	Mud Springs.

NAME.	Age	Place of Nativity.	Occupation.	Local Residence.
Deihl, Ephraim	24	Ohio	Miner	Georgetown.
Divata, Antonio	32	Italy	"	Newtown.
Doan, Robert	32	Canada	Farmer	Latrobe.
Dickinson, David Porter	44	Massachusetts	"	Kelsey.
Dolong, Alva	38	Vermont	Miner	Georgetown.
Doncaster, Samuel	32	Pennsylvania	Bricklayer	"
Darling, Alfred	43	Massachusetts	Farmer	Garden Valley.
Doss, Joel Wilson	31	Indiana	Landlord	Lake Valley.
Dean, Samuel	29	Indiana	Laborer	" "
Drinkwater, Addison	42	Maine	Miner	White Oak Township.
Davenport, Horace	56	New York	Carpenter	Salmon Falls Township.
Doncaster, Richard, jr	37	Pennsylvania	Miner	Kelsey "
Denuth, Geo. Washington	30	Michigan	"	" "
Dryden, Nathaniel B	34	Missouri	"	" "
Davis, Harrison Osborn	34	Virginia	Road Overseer	" "
Dodd, John Henry	36	New Jersey	Miner	" "
Derringer, Lemuel	34	Ohio	"	Diamond Springs.
Dresser, Rufus	51	Massachusetts	Carpenter	" "
Dutton, John Bliss	41	Vermont	Farmer	Fair Play.
Dale, Phillip Augustus	45	Massachusetts	"	Coyoteville.
Daywalt, George	55	Pennsylvania	Miner	Indian Diggings
Davis, William Wilson	51	North Carolina	Laborer	" "
Dille, Joseph Barr	33	Ohio	Miner	Fair Play.
Dunn, Joseph McDonald	37	Virginia	"	Indian Diggings.
Davis, John Wills	47	Massachusetts	Farmer	Pilot Hill.
Davis, William Russell	36	Massachusetts	Miner	Spanish Dry Diggings.
Davis, Alfred Bronson	31	Massachusetts	"	Greenwood.
Dolley, George Hoyte	39	Maine	"	Pilot Hill.
Durgin, Trueworthy	47	N. Hampshire	"	Spanish Dry Diggings.
Duncan, Richard Henry	42	Virginia	Merchant	Duncan's Store.
Davidson, Thomas	39	New York	Toll Road Keep	Buckeye Flat.
Davis, Bela Fitch	41	Maine	Laborer	El Dorado.
Deackins, William Henry	31	Tennessee	Saloon-keeper	"
Donahoe, Thomas	37	Delaware	Butcher	Latrobe.
Dean, James Edward	30	Massachusetts	Cook	Placerville.
Donahoe, James	41	Ireland	Miner	Kelsey.
Dunahoo, William Wash	39	North Carolina	Ditch Agent	Georgetown.
Ditson, William	52	Massachusetts	Farmer	Placerville.
Dyball, James	47	England	Miner	Georgetown.
Dutry, Manuel	40	Peak Pico, W.I	"	" "
Dunham, John Sheppard	61	New Jersey	"	" "
Delwich, Henry	39	Germany	"	" "
Day, Thomas	33	Ireland	"	White Oak.
Dreier, Henry	39	Prussia	Butcher	" "
Day, Dorance	33	Maine	Farmer	Salmon Falls.
Dorrington, Levi	23	England	"	" "
Duden, Calvin William	29	Ohio	Railroad Agent	Mud Springs Township
Dicks, Cassius M. Clay	23	Ohio	Farmer	" " "
Dunn, James Wesley	36	Kentucky	Laborer	" " "
Doan, Elisha	72	Massachusetts	Miner	" " "
Donavan, Michael D	40	Ireland	"	" " "
Duke, George Terry	40	Great Britain	"	" " "
Davis, Samuel French	37	Maine	"	Grizzly Flat.
Diewald, Mathias	44	Germany	"	Cosumnes Township.
Davis, Edward	35	England	"	White Oak "
Devine, Charles	26	Louisiana	"	Mud Springs.
Duckworth, Edward	38	England	Teamster	" "
Delawney, F. Bourdenier	31	Maryland	Cook	" "
Degleman, John, jr	32	Germany	Shoemaker	Placerville.
Davidson, Milford	42	New York	Miner	Diamond Springs.
Davison, Thomas	27	Massachusetts	"	White Oak.
Delfoch, Bernardo	25	Switzerland	"	Diamond Springs.
Debernardo, Jacom	22	Switzerland	"	Placerville.

NAME.	Age	Place of Nativity.	Occupation.	Local Residence.
Davey, Henry Hasking	22	England	Farmer	Placerville.
Draier, Jacob	29	Germany	"	Greenwood.
Deller, Andrew	55	Bavaria	Miner	"
Debernardi, Giulio	23	Switzerland	"	Diamond Springs T'p.
Dale, Abraham Creek	36	Missouri	"	Placerville.
Drummond, Archibald N.	59	Kentucky	"	Georgetown Township.
Durgan, William Berry	54	Virginia	Teamster	" "
Dailey, John William	50	Maryland	Miner	" "
Dater, Robert	50	New York	"	Placerville "
Drewery, Raffail	59	Illinois	"	Diamond Springs T'p.
Denio, John	43	Vermont	Farmer	" " "
Dunning, Henry	39	Vermont	"	" " "
Dougherty, Alexander	25	Missouri	Miner	" " "
Devoll, Gideon	45	Massachusetts	Farmer	Uniontown.
Delorey, Edman	38	Massachusetts	"	Coloma.
Dalzell, David Fisher	49	New Jersey	Hotel keeper	Shingle Springs.
Davenport, John Lilburn	31	Virginia	Miner	Latrobe.
Davis, Stephen Nelvil	42	Pennsylvania	Engineer	"
Daniels, Russell Brace	38	New York	Miner	Brownsville.
Driver, Achilles Thomas	44	Virginia	"	Fair Play.
Delavan, James Lawrence	57	Pennsylvania	"	White Oak Township.
Dick, Samuel Rigart	36	Ohio	Carpenter	" "
Davis, Thos. Sam. Smith	44	Indiana	Laborer	" "
Daggett, Zenes	60	Maine	Miner	Kelsey "
Duvall, Geo. Washington	63	Maryland	"	" "
Dickinson, Fred. Goderd	45	Massachusetts	"	" "
Dennis, Henry Franklin	40	Rhode Island	"	" "
Day, Samuel Aston	24	Ohio	Farmer	" "
Davis, Daniel	47	New York	Miner	Greenwood.
De Haven, James	26	Illinois	Hostler	Dick Ranch.
Dobson, Joseph	29	Illinois	Miner	Placerville.
Dowdy, Hiram Kingston	35	Kentucky	"	Georgetown.
Devenny, James	36	Ohio	"	"
Dingley, William Henry	42	Maine	"	"
Daniels, Stephen Ruddie	32	Missouri	"	Pleasant Valley.
Daniels, Francis Riffle	28	Missouri	"	" "
Dean, John Jacob	38	Germany	Merchant	El Dorado.
Day, John Calvin	34	Ohio	Farmer	Kelsey Township.
Davis, James	39	Ireland	Miner	Georgetown.
Davey, William	35	England	"	"
Debernardi, John	21	Switzerland	Teamster	Placerville.
Dodson, Marcus	36	Kentucky	Farmer	Mud Springs.
Dodd, Alex. Butterfield	29	New York	Laborer	Lake Valley Township.
Dorr, Arthur Wellington	39	Maine	Carpenter	" "
Dillon, Larkin Woody	35	Virginia	Stage Driver	" "
Decon, William	35	Ohio	Miner	Placerville.
Delong, Nicholas Melton	28	Indiana	Rancher	Shingle Springs.
Davis, John	63	Virginia	Painter	Latrobe.
Dobbas, Joseph	33	Switzerland	Butcher	Georgetown.
Dobbas, Cherubino	27	Switzerland	"	"
Davis, John	42	Great Britain	Miner	Placerville.
Dean, James Edward	29	Massachusetts	"	" Township.

E

Eisfeldt, Theodore, Sr.	52	Germany	Miner	Placerville.
Eisfeldt, Theodore, Jr.	31	Germany	Musician	"
Evison, Ole	36	Norway	Miner	Indian Diggings.
Egleston, Morris	39	New York	"	Uniontown.
Ensminger, Samuel James	51	Virginia	City Marshal	Placerville.
Ebernz, Blassins	46	Germany	Mason	"
Elmendrof, Dumont	47	New Jersey	Laborer	"
Eidinger, Augustus	35	Germany	Farmer	"
Ellis, Daniel Asbey	41	Kentucky	Miner	Kelsey.

NAME.	Age	Place of Nativity.	Occupation.	Local Residence.
Engesser, Phillip	33	Germany	Teamster	Placerville.
Evins, Jehu	40	Delaware	Laborer	"
Eddy, Isaac	36	Illinois	Speculator	"
Elliot, John	33	Pennsylvania	Miner	"
Evans, James Powell	29	Missouri	"	"
Ellicott, Andrew	41	New York	"	Smith's Flat.
Elrod, Edward Raymond	40	Indiana	"	" "
Ely, Thomas Benjamin	31	Missouri	"	Placerville.
Edgerton, Calvin	26	Vermont	Attorney	"
Eastwood, Morris Seely	35	Ohio	Miner	Diamond Springs.
Eubanks, David King	25	Missouri	"	Placerville.
Endriss, George David	38	Germany	"	Michigan Flat.
Eaton, Joseph	50	Georgia	"	Georgetown Township.
Ellinwood, Tilden Bradley	44	Massachusetts	Farmer	Diamond Springs.
Epley, John Wesley	29	New York	Miner	Placerville Township.
Eddy, John	26	Illinois	Farmer	" "
Evans, Edward Harland	39	Maryland	Miner	Diamond Springs.
Erickson, Erick	39	Norway	"	Cosumnes Township.
Eggleston, Joshua	28	Vermont	Lumberman	Georgetown Township.
Einsfield, Casper	34	Prussia	Miner	Fair Play.
England, Marion	33	Tennessee	"	Georgetown.
Evans, James	45	Massachusetts	Cooper	Volcanoville.
Errine, David	37	Missouri	Miner	Kelsey Township.
Eckman, Elias	33	Maryland	"	Diamond Springs.
Edner, Henry	50	Missouri	Blacksmith	Brownsville.
Edmondson, Jonathan	34	Ohio	Merchant	Indian Diggings.
Eagleson, Alexander	37	Virginia	Wheelwright	Pilot Hill.
Edgerton, George Eddy	37	Vermont	Carpenter	" "
Evans, Thomas Blakelen	41	Massachusetts	Miner	Greenwood.
Edsall, Walter Joseph	36	Canada	Farmer	Kelsey Township.
Envert, Charles	41	Denmark	Miner	Georgetown.
Edmondson, John Wesley	39	Illinois	"	"
Ebbert, Louis	33	Pennsylvania	Farmer	White Oak.
Egelston, James Henry	34	Kentucky	Miner	" "
Edwards, Peter	47	Sweden	Laborer	Mud Springs.
Eycleshimer, J. Rowland	35	New York	Wagon-maker	" "
Eppinger, Jacob	30	Germany	Merchant	" "
Etchels, Joseph	34	England	Miner	" "
Egbert, Christopher H	31	Missouri	Laborer	Mountain Township.
Eckholm, Tobias William	45	Finland	Miner	Cosumnes "
Easton, Thomas William	43	England	Hotel-keeper	" "
Evan, John	38	Holland	Merchant	White Oak "
Ellis, Spencer Crocket	50	Virginia	Laborer	Placerville.
Ehat, Caspar	47	Germany	Saloon keeper	Diamond Springs.
Everts, Thomas	35	Massachusetts	Farmer	Placerville.
Exline, Burnard	46	Pennsylvania	Miner	Grizzly Flat.
Eitzell, Conrad	43	Germany	Farmer	White Oak.
Emery, Jessee Burnham	38	Maine	Carpenter	Placerville.
Evora, Jose	44	Mexico	Miner	"
Evans, James Low	46	Massachusetts	Cooper	Volcanoville.
Ells, George Sherman	39	New York	Miner	Diamond Springs.
Ellis, Benjamin	23	New York	Farmer	Coloma.
Edward, Guyself	42	Kentucky	Wagon-maker	Shingle Springs.
Eversole, James	35	Ohio	Butcher	Mountain.
Edmunds, Benjamin Free	42	U. S.	Miner	Coloma.
Epps, Tinsley Burton	30	North Carolina	"	Georgetown.
Ellen, Elle	44	Germany	"	Mud Springs.
Ells, Verrannus	39	Massachusetts	"	White Oak Township.
Ensey, John Campbell	57	Maryland	Saloon-keeper	Mud Springs.
Ellis, Jack Sargent	38	Vermont	Dairyman	Lake Valley.
Eastbrook, James Kimball	53	Maine	Miner	Greenwood.
Eames, Manly	63	Maine	News Agent	Latrobe.
Eckel, Henry Snyder	28	Pennsylvania	Miner	Mud Springs.

NAMES.	Age	Place of Nativity.	Occupation.	Local Residence.
Edwards, Arthur William	21	New York	Farmer	Shingle Springs.
Eddings, William "C"	27	Illinois	Carpenter	Mud Springs.
Ellis, George Riley	36	Maine	Minister	"
Ebert, William	34	Germany	Farmer	White Oak Township.
Etzel, Jacob	24	Germany	"	" "
Eastman, Melatiah Willis	27	Vermont	Laborer	Placerville "
Evans, Daniel McLane	33	Illinois	Hostler	" "
Elkin, William Thomas	31	Illinois	Clerk	" "
Ellicot, John	32	New York	Water Agent	" "

F

NAMES.	Age	Place of Nativity.	Occupation.	Local Residence.
Fisk, Ira Almirin	52	Ohio	Farmer	White Oak Township.
Fitch, George Clinton	41		"	" "
Foster, Theron	54	Massachusetts	"	" "
Fink, Francis	50	Prussia	Saloon-keeper	Placerville.
Farrell, William Briten	38	Kentucky	"	"
Fraser, Thomas	33	Great Britain	Merchant	"
Frank, Frederick	40	Germany	Miner	Clarksville.
Foster, Chas. Thompson	36	Kentucky	Water Agent	Mud Springs.
Fox, John	35	Ohio	Blacksmith	Placerville.
Frees, William Henry	39	Maine	Farmer	"
Fletcher, Thomas Mason	39	New York	Laborer	"
Fairbanks, George	42	Indiana	Farmer	"
Fairbanks, Hiram	62	N. Hampshire	"	"
Fowler, Thomas Sewell	43	New York	Carpenter	"
Fitch, Halsey	31	Ohio	Quartz Miner	"
Foxwell, Jonathan	35	Illinois	Engineer	" Township.
Francis, Joseph	44	Massachusetts	Miner	" "
Fannin, Henry William	35	New York	School teacher	Diamond Springs.
Foster, Johnson William	53	Maine	Farmer	Placerville.
Francis, George	44	Greece	Merchant	"
Fleming, Martin	40	Ireland	Miner	Coloma.
Foster, James Henry	27	Maine	Farmer	Placerville.
Freyer, Samuel John	36	England	Miner	" Township.
Friedel, John	32	Bavaria	"	Michigan Flat.
Faber, Frederick	62	Denmark	Farmer	White Oak Township.
Faber, William Walfred	22	Denmark	"	" "
Fockler, James	37	Pennsylvania	Miner	Georgetown "
Fleming, Peter	43	Germany	"	White Oak "
Figuera, Louis	44	Virginia	Cabinet-maker	Placerville "
Fink, Jacob Frederick	48	Germany	Miner	Shingle Springs.
Fisher, Daniel	33	Germany	Baker	Placerville.
Ferguson, Wm. Sinclair	42	Kentucky	Farmer	Mountain Township.
Fouke, William Davis	29	Maryland	Miner	White Oak "
Fraso, Joseph	48	Massachusetts	Farmer	Coloma.
Frame, Iames Smith	44	Ohio	"	Placerville Township.
Fiske, Lucius Colwell	53	Massachusetts	Miner	" "
Furst, Nathan	25	Bavaria	Book-keeper	"
Foutch, James Monroe	46	Ohio	Farmer	Diamond Springs T'p.
Foote, William	40	New York	Road Overseer	" "
Fleming, Albert Carlisle	24	Illinois	Lumberman	" "
Fleming, Charles Edgar	21	Illinois	"	" "
Fleming, Thomas Robert	27	Illinois	"	" "
Fleming, John	37	Delaware	Hotel Keeper	" "
Fredericks, Charles	59	Hanover	Physician	Georgetown Township
Fenton, Fenjamin	36	New York	Miner	Greenwood "
Fuller, Hiram Henry	36	New York	Livery	Georgetown "
Farnsworth, J. Franklin	27	Virginia	"	" "
Fox, Daniel William	40	Connecticut	Farmer	" "
Fountain, Garret Wash'n	46	New York	Landlord	Lake Valley "
Fraser, Hugh Harrison	26	Ohio	Clerk	Salmon Falls "
Foster, William Henry	40	Maine	Farmer	Kelsey "
Frost, Amos Locke	41	Massachusetts	Miner	" "

Name.	Age	Place of Nativity.	Occupation.	Local Residence.
Frazer, Maryland Skinner	52	Maryland	Saloon-keeper	Kelsey Township.
Ford, Simeon Jasper	38	Tennessee	Ditch Agent	Brownsville.
Felker, Geo. Washington	53	Pennsylvania	Farmer	Coyoteville.
Felker, William	26	Wisconsin	"	"
Funk, Martin Mortimer	36	Ohio	Ditch Agent	Fair Play.
Forbes, Benjamin	26	New York	Miner	Indian Diggings.
Ford, George	41	Ohio	"	Fair Play.
Farnsworth, John Benj'n	37	Vermont	Farmer	Coyoteville.
Frey, William	44	Missouri	Miner	Brownsville.
Freeman, Enoch George	36	Maine	"	Greenwood.
Ferree, Geo. Washington	35	Indiana	"	"
Ferguson, D. H. Cumpton	28	Missouri	"	Pilot Hill.
Ferguson, Newton John	37	Ohio	"	Spanish Dry Diggings.
Fox, Hiram Wellington	40	Vermont	"	Pilot Hill.
Ferguson, Thomas, Sr.	67	Pennsylvania	Farmer	" "
Ferguson, Hugh Jackson	31	Georgia	Miner	Smith's Flat.
Freeland, George Davis	29	New York	Wheelwright	Shingle Springs.
Finley, James	48	Kentucky	Wine Grower	Cosumnes Township.
Fitz Gibbons, Thomas	31	Michigan	Butcher	El Dorado.
Fleishman, Jacob	37	Bohemia	Merchant	Greenwood.
Foutch, Abraham	34	Ohio	W'd & Coal Dl'r	Diamond Springs Tp.
Finnon, James	41	Ireland	Laborer	Kelsey.
Flora, And'w Washington	35	Wisconsin	Miner	Georgetown Township.
Finnon, Christopher	39	Ireland	Farmer	Kelsey "
Frees, John Frederick	51	Hanover	Miner	" "
Fraser, David	43	Vermont	"	Georgetown "
Foley, Thomas	68	Ireland	Gardener	" "
Fortune, William	45	North Carolina	Miner	"
Flinn, John	40	Ireland	"	"
Franklin, James	26	Indiana	"	" "
Fargo, Thomas Turner	39	Pennsylvania	"	Greenwood.
Frisby, Henry Clay	34	Kentucky	Butcher	Salmon Falls.
Fruth, Frederick	41	Bavaria	Farmer	Coloma.
Frahm, Hinrich Frederick	42	Denmark	"	"
Fredman, John	46	Germany	"	White Oak Township.
Franklin, Quintis L. C.	42	Georgia	Miner	" "
Forrester, Paul	41	Germany	"	" "
Frers, Henry Harmen	46	Hanover	"	" "
Ford, George Washington	35	Pennsylvania	Clerk	Mud Springs.
Foley, Morris	25	Ireland	Farmer	" "
Fisher, Joseph	40	Germany	"	White Oak Township.
Freeman, Albert	37	New York	Miner	Mud Springs.
Frochlick, John	53	Baden	"	Cosumnes Township.
Fagin, Henry	50	Germany	Farmer	Diamond Springs.
Fleming, Samuel	52	Delaware	Toll Keeper	" "
Fackner, William	40	Germany	Miner	Mud "
Fass, William	38	Prussia	Farmer	Diamond "
Fowler, John Sherman	23	Massachusetts	Teamster	" "
Fisk, Almerin	60	Vermont	Miner	Placerville.
Flinn, William Jurdan	40	Tennessee	Millman	Diamond Springs.
Fairbanks, George	43	Indiana	Laborer	Placerville.
Fortunato, Boldrini	53	Austria	Saloon-keeper	" Township.
Fink, Charles	29	Baden	Butcher	Diamond Springs Tp.
Flynn, Dennis	29	Ireland	Farmer	Placerville "
Fisher, Frank	50	Switzerland	"	Mud Springs "
Fink, John	33	Baden	Butcher	Diamond Springs.
Flinn, Patrick	47	Ireland	Miner	Georgetown.
Farwell, Samuel Day	38	Ohio	"	Gold Hill.
Fonkermeier, Herman	44	Prussia	"	" "
Freberger, Joseph	25	France	"	Mud Springs.
Fugate, Robert Colbert	36	Virginia	"	Gold Hill.
Forbes, James Olmsted	53	Ohio	Farmer	Georgetown.
Ferguson, Newton John	37	Ohio	Carpenter	"

NAME.	Age	Place of Nativity.	Occupation.	Local Residence.
Francis, David Jones	48	Pennsylvania	Miner	Georgetown.
Farnsworth, John Calvin	38	Virginia	"	Georgetown Township.
Flora, John Jackson	33	Ohio	"	" "
Franklin, James Henry	34	Ohio	"	Diamond Springs.
Foutch, John	31	Ohio	Wood Chopper	" "
Frost, Ephraim Sheldon	55	Massachusetts	Farmer	Coloma.
Foss, Ivery Lock	33	North Carolina	Carpenter	Nashville.
Foster, William	56	Pennsylvania	Ditch Agent	Cosumnes Township.
Ford, William	21	Iowa	Dairyman	White Oak Township.
Freeman, Samuel	50	New York	Farmer	" " "
Ferguson, James Falls	40	Tennessee	Ditch Agent	" " "
Freel, James Washington	37	Illinois	Miner	" " "
Fargo, Tracy Turner	35	Pennsylvania	"	Spanish Dry Diggings.
Fenton, Elbridge Gerry	27	New York	"	Greenwood.
Freeman, Geo. Washingt'n	37	Tennessee	"	Placerville.
Fesper, John	31	Ohio	"	"
Fowler, Stephen Budwick	26	Maine	"	Mountain Township.
Frye, Alphonzo Gerrish	31	Maine	"	" "
Fowler, Henry Pinkney	37	Arkansas	"	" "
Fisher, Jacob Bolton	31	Virginia	"	" "
Fisher, George	45	Germany	Farmer	White Oak "
Frater, Geo. Washington	38	Scotland	Miner	Kelsey "
Fewell, James Madison	41	Tennessee	"	Georgetown "
Folsom, James Madison	37	Indiana	"	" "
Filson, McKneal	55	Virginia	"	Diamond Springs.
Fenstell, Ed. Albert Gus	51	Hanover	Farmer	Gold Hill.
Forbes, James Olmstead	53	Vermont	"	Georgetown Township.
Fairchilds, Ebenezer	44	Indiana	Carpenter	Salmon Falls "
Ferguson, Thomas, Jr	31	Missouri	Miner	Pilot Hill "
Farnsworth, Seba	62	Massachusetts	Farmer	" "
Fegley, Jacob	48	Pennsylvania	Miner	Placerville.
Fuller, Lewis Harrison	56	Ohio	Farmer	Grizzly Flat.
Follis, William Riley	45	Tennessee	Teamster	White Oak.
Forrester, Geo. H. Hutch	50	Massachusetts	Barkeeper	Shingle Springs.
Fralich, David Douglass	43	New York	Laborer	Latrobe.
Feltz, Jesse	40	Ohio	Teamster	El Dorado.
Fransioli, Ant. Alessander	29	Switzerland	Butcher	Georgetown.
Fair, William	59	Scotland	Carpenter	"
Flansburg, Philo	28	New York	Lumberman	Placerville Township.

G

NAME.	Age	Place of Nativity.	Occupation.	Local Residence.
Griffith, Maurice Griffith	39	Pennsylvania	Sheriff	Diamond Springs.
Giles, John W. Sum'rhays	40	New York	Farmer	Clarksville.
Gaylord, William Elijah	44	Connecticut	"	Weber Creek Bridge.
Griffin, Frank	33	New York	"	Rose Spring.
Gibbs, Edward Chase	27	Massachusetts	Miner	White Oak Township.
Gardner, Benjamin Allen	49	Massachusetts	"	" " "
Gilmore, Canada	45	Ohio	"	" " "
Gray, Young	50	Kentucky	Farmer	" " "
Gray, Allen Taylor	51	Illinois	"	" " "
Gray, Owen Asbel	23	Illinois	Miner	" " "
Gray, Dallas Polk	22	Illinois	"	" " "
Griffin, James	29	Missouri	"	Placerville "
Gillinwater, Thos. Adams	49	Tennessee	Carpenter	Placerville.
Giffen, Geo. Washington	35	Illinois	Miner	Coloma Township.
Gavin, Barney	27	Ireland	"	Diamond Springs.
Gallahan, John Alexander	40	Ohio	"	" "
Gelwicks, Daniel William	44	Maryland	Printer	Placerville.
Goodnow, Albert Lincoln	45	Massachusetts	Miner	Coloma Township.
Glover, William	46	Massachusetts	"	Placerville "
Goen, Noah Hale	34	N. Hampshire	Machinist	Mud Sp'gs "
Gaterman, Hans Henry	50	Germany	Painter	Placerville "

NAME.	Age	Place of Nativity.	Occupation.	Local Residence.
Gould, William	32	New York	Gardner	Coloma Township.
Gelatt, Wallace "W"	28	New York	Tinsmith	Placerville "
Glackin, Edward	30	Ireland	Miner	Coloma "
Green, Geo. Washington	24	Wisconsin	"	Placerville "
Gilbert, Martin Saulsbury	35	New York	Farmer	Diamond Springs Tp.
Gildea, Charles	30	Ireland	Tailor	Placerville "
Gumpper, John	34	Germany	Bootmaker	Diamond Springs Tp.
Goings, Elisha	33	Pennsylvania	Miner	Placerville "
Gillett, Thomas Jefferson	63	New York	Farmer	" "
Green, George W	54	New York	Civil Engineer	" "
Glynn, Ira	68	Vermont	Dentist	" "
Green, Benjamin	57	Kentucky	Shoemaker	"
Gignac, Lewis Henry	22	Ohio	Miner	"
Gates, Corydon	47	Massachusetts	Shoemaker	"
Gifford, L. Washburn	32	Massachusetts	Miner	"
Gardner, Pliny	35	Massachusetts	"	"
Gills, John King	38	Ohio	Teamster	"
Grotheer, Martin	37	Hanover	Farmer	Michigan Flat.
Graner, Charles	42	Germany	"	Coloma Township.
Golden, Julius	37	Prussia	Merchant	Placerville.
Gillett, Marinos	36	Ohio	Writ'g Teacher	"
Griffith, John	34	Wales	Lawyer	Georgetown.
Goyan, Frank	32	England	Miner	Placerville.
Gale, Gilbert	22	New York	Toll Collector	"
Gray, Alexander	36	Scotland	Miner	" Township.
Glassman, Jacob	34	France	Merchant	Georgetown.
Gallaher, Wm. Randolph	32	Virginia	Farmer	Uniontown.
Green, Nathaniel	55	Virginia	Miner	Cosumnes Township.
Gardella, Andrea	25	Italy	Merchant	Newtown.
Green, Benjamin Franklin	29	Wisconsin	Miner	Placerville.
Gamble, Andrew Jackson	29	Illinois	Teamster	" Township.
Gurney, Daniel Porter	29	Maine	Millwright	" "
Gignac, Leander	47	Lower Canada	Miner	" "
Galiner, Nicholas Gazway	28	Ohio	Farmer	Diamond Springs.
Guffy, William Georgia	33	Ohio	Miner	" "
Gentry, Thomas	31	Kentucky	"	" "
Gardner, Charles Avery	38	Connecticut	Farmer	" "
Garvitt, Elijah Worth'gt'n	56	Connecticut	"	Placerville Township.
Giddings, John	33	Connecticut	Laborer	" "
Grainger, Juan Fernandez	24	Kentucky	Miner	Shingle Springs.
Greenwood, Edmund	40	Pennsylvania	"	Placerville Township.
Gilliland, Jno. McChesney	32	Pennsylvania	"	Georgetown "
Gillpatric, George	75	Maine	"	" "
Green, Lyman Francis	33	Massachusetts	Machinist	" "
Gibbs, William Thomas	37	Missouri	Blacksmith	" "
Gardiner, Andw. Boynton	43	Massachusetts	Hotel-keeper	Lake Valley "
Gibbs, William	44	Massachusetts	Farmer	Uniontown.
Gasberie, Louis	62	New York	Ranch'r & Miner	Kelsey Township.
Gay, Ambrose Cushman	49	Connecticut	Hotel-keeper	Diamond Springs.
George, Lawrence Mitch	56	Virginia	Farmer	"
Gillmore, Joseph Grant	36	Indiana	Miner	Cosumnes Township.
Gorman, Richard	45	New York	"	Pilot Hill.
George, Evan	34	Pennsylvania	Farmer	Greenwood.
Gould, John Lewis	21	Illinois	"	Pilot Hill.
Galt, Thomas Augustus	36	South Carolina	Miner	Diamond Springs Tp.
Goldy, James Durham	40	Pennsylvania	"	Logtown.
Gray, William Hoxey	45	Illinois	"	Kelly Flat.
Gitchell, Daniel Bennett	44	New York	Blacksmith	Georgetown.
Giamboni, Joseph	51	Switzerland	Glazier	Placerville Township.
Gallaher, Nael	55	Ireland	Miner	Kelsey "
Giroux, Henry	38	Great Britain	Blacksmith	Georgetown "
Giroux, Leon George	30	Canada	Miner	" "
Green, Charles	47	Portugal	Gardener	" "

NAME.	Age	Place of Nativity.	Occupation.	Local Residence.
Gusio, John	33	Switzerland	Merchant	Greenwood.
Gallagher, Francis	44	Ireland	Miner	Coloma.
Gale, George	37	England	Farmer	"
Grainger, Marion Selkirk	22	Kentucky	Miner	Mud Springs Township
Gallagher, Thomas	39	Ireland	"	White Oak Township.
Gibbs, George Sheffield	34	Massachusetts	"	" " "
Gains, John William	42	Great Britain	"	Salmon Falls Township.
Gallagher, Hugh	56	Ireland	Farmer	" "
Grace, Timothy	47	Virginia	"	" "
Grace, John	21	Indiana	Teamster	" "
Godard, John	40	Arkansas	Miner	Mud Springs Township.
Gottch, Claus	46	Denmark	"	" "
Griggs, George	40	Massachusetts	Forw'ing Ag't	" "
Graham, Andrew Jackson	35	New York	Miner	Grizzly Flat.
Garland, Thomas	68	Ireland	"	"
Gunn, Philip	40	Ireland	"	"
Griffin, James Riley	40	Ohio	Farmer	"
Geislor, Lorens	54	Hanover	Miner	Cosumnes Township.
Gaywood, James	33	Germany	"	Georgetown.
Guibenheimer, Frederick	38	Germany	Brewer	Placerville.
Gillard, John Montgomery	36	New York	Hotel Keeper	Lake Valley Township
Godfrey, Jonathan	40	New York	Laborer	Placerville Township.
Gross, Jakob	32	Bavaria	Brewer	Mud Springs "
Gilbert, James	36	Ireland	Miner	Placerville "
Giudici, Francisco	45	Switzerland	Farmer	Diamond Springs T'p.
Gray, John	38	England	Miner	Coloma Township.
Graham, Levi Allen	31	Canada	"	Placerville Township.
Gerbode, Franz	41	Hanover	"	Kelsey Township.
Giamboni, Frank Natel	30	New York	"	Placerville Township.
Gudolard, August	45	Switzerland	"	Coloma "
Gruber, Claus Henry	40	Hanover	Farmer	" "
Gensen, Mathias	51	Denmark	Miner	" "
Gilman, Sewell Joshua	28	Maine	"	Georgetown "
Graves, John Langley	54	Delaware	"	" "
Gould, William Albert	33	Michigan	"	Diamond Springs T'p.
Gipe, David William	37	Pennsylvania	"	" " "
Gray, Robert Johnson	21	Arkansas	"	" " "
Gallagher, John	29	New York	Farmer	Coloma Township.
Gray, Asbell Alexander	22	Kentucky	Miner	El Dorado.
Gilmore, Nathan	36	Ohio	Farmer	"
Geer, Norman John	33	Ohio	Miner	"
Grant, John Dyer	28	Missouri	"	Nashville.
Gardiner, George Bently	50	Rhode Island	Farmer	El Dorado.
Grist, Jacob	47	Pennsylvania	"	Shingle Springs.
Grimes, James "S"	34	Ohio	Teamster	" "
Galweth, Gabriel	40	Maryland	Miner	Nashville.
Gibson, Patrick	45	Missouri	"	Brownsville,
Gray, John	32	Missouri	"	Fair Play.
Gafney, James	35	Ireland	Butcher	Shingle Springs.
Grandy, Alonzo Henry	34	New York	Miner	White Oak Township.
Grover, Melvin Lincoln	36	Maine	Farmer	Kelsey "
Golden, Daniel	34	Massachusetts	"	" "
Goodpasture, George	29	Ohio	Miner	Pilot Hill.
Gilbert, Ephram Crocket	56	Kentucky	Farmer	Salmon Falls Township
Gilbert, Delano Eckles	37	Indiana	"	" " "
Gilbert, Hiram Harrison	30	Indiana	"	" " "
Gallagher, Peter	41	Great Britain	Miner	Diamond Springs T'p.
Gray, Baker Thomas	26	New York	Teamster	Placerville.
Gilmore, Robert	40	N. Hampshire	Blacksmith	"
Griggs, Thomas Young	37	Illinois	Farmer	"
Galbreth, David Arthur	31	Missouri	Miner	Mountain Township.
Griffin, James Riley	40	Ohio	"	" "
Gamblin, Joseph	38	Georgia	"	" "

NAMES.	Age	Place of Nativity.	Occupation.	Local Residence.
Guiselman, Joseph Henry	32	Indiana	Miner	Mountain Township.
Gafney, Nicholas	30	Virginia	"	Mud Springs Township.
Gilbert, Ches. Crittenden	34	Michigan	Farmer	Diamond Springs "
Gregery, William Albert	35	Missouri	Shingle-maker	" " "
Goodrich, Charles Barnes	31	Illinois	Miner	Placerville "
Graham, John	53	Ireland	Hotel-keeper	White Oak "
Golen, Valentine	51	Switzerland	Miner	Placerville "
Gusati, Silvester	39	Switzerland	"	Diamond Springs "
Graser, John	47	Bavaria	Farmer	Georgetown "
Gilmer, Andrew	49	Ireland	Teamster	Placerville "
Groover, Samuel	27	England	Farmer	Coloma "
Gregor, William	24	Ireland	Miner	Placerville "
Gates, John Francis	38	Connecticut	Teamster	Georgetown.
Gardner, Ezekiel Congdon	51	Rhode Island	Miner	Georgetown.
Gibbs, David Asbery	38	North Carolina	Laborer	Lake Valley Township.
Grout, John Henry	38	Massachusetts	Miner	Greenwood "
Grinnell, William Henry	41	New York	"	" "
Gressim, Wilson Turner	41	Tennessee	"	Grizzly Flat.
Grimes, George	42	Ohio	Farmer	Shingle Springs.
Given, Isaac Langdon	50	Ohio	Miner	El Dorado.
Green, William Alfred	47	Kentucky	"	Latrobe.
Griffith, Wm. E. Carson	50	Tennessee	Blacksmith	El Dorado.
Grace, James Thomas	38	Maryland	Blacksmith	Shingle Springs.
Goodwin, John	37	Illinois	Laborer	Latrobe.
Glines, Sumner	32	N. Hampshire	Farmer	El Dorado.
Greet, William	32	Massachusetts	Laborer	"
Gleason, Samuel Larison	59	Massachusetts	Miner	"
Goodpasture, Amos	50	Ohio	Laborer	Mud Springs.
Gardner, William	31	Ireland	Miner	Fair Play.
Goss, Joseph Harvy	35	Kentucky	Road Agent	Placerville Township.

H

NAMES.	Age	Place of Nativity.	Occupation.	Local Residence.
Henry, Ashmer Cook	37	Ohio	Merchant	Placerville.
Hornblower, Frederick A.	39	England	Lawyer	"
Holdridge, Louis	54	New York	Farmer	White Oak Township.
Hall, William Jackson	23	Illinois	Teamster	" " "
Hitchens, John	51	England	Miner	Kelsey "
Henderson, William	69	Pennsylvania	Surveyor	Placerville "
Hall, James Queen	34	North Carolina	Miner	Coloma.
Hicks, Constantine	48	Vermont	Carpenter	Salmon Falls "
Hanley, Dennis	34	Missouri	Ditch Agent	Kelsey "
Hardie, Thomas	73	Great Britain	Gentleman	Placerville "
Hogsett, Thomas	40	Ireland	Baker	" "
Howard, Asb. Armstrong	42	Indiana	Farmer	" "
Halftermeyer, Amand	53	France	"	" "
Hume, James Bunyan	38	New York	Under Sheriff	" "
Hickok, Oliver Henry	36	Vermont	Laborer	" "
Hooper, William Henry	34	Ohio	Farmer	Coloma "
Hanrahan, Michael	35	Ireland	Stonecutter	Diamond Springs T'p.
Hamel, Henry	33	Germany	Butcher	Placerville.
Haskins, Charles Warren	41	Massachusetts	Rancher	Smith's Flat.
Hare, Andrew Jackson	27	Ohio	Teacher	Rose Springs.
Hunger, August	30	France	Butcher	Placerville.
Hunger, Frederick	35	France	Butcher	"
Hoxie, Peleg Pitman	49	Rhode Island	Gardener	"
Huck, Vorman	49	Germany	Butcher	"
Hilbert, Charles	38	Germany	Hotel keeper	"
Hennessy, Patrick	45	Ireland	Miner	Coloma.
Hume, Robert	36	Ireland	"	"
Highland, John	35	Ireland	Farmer	Placerville.
Hinchman, Andrew Lewis	29	Virginia	Carpenter	"
Hopper, Levi Isaac	33	New York	Mason	"

NAME.	Age	Place of Nativity.	Occupation.	Local Residence.
Hoffman, Martin Luther..	27	Illinois	Wine-grower	Placerville.
Hooper, Henry Otis	43	Massachusetts	Dr & sash mkr.	Diamond Springs T'p.
Hittinger, Charles	38	Germany	Butcher	" "
Herrill, Eli	38	Tennessee	Farmer	Placerville Township.
Howard, Amos	34	Maine	Hotel-keeper	" "
Hart, Charles	61	Connecticut	Farmer	" "
Humsberger, Levi	50	Pennsylvania	"	" "
Hulburd, Byron Horatio.	21	Wisconsin	"	" "
House, William Betine	37	New York	"	" "
Hinkley, Oliver	36	Maine	Agt Pioneer St.	" "
Hulburd, Hiland Smith	47	Vermont	Farmer	" "
Hamilton, N. Augustus	31	New York	Attorney	" "
Hall, Isaac	41	Pennsylvania	Carpenter	" "
Howlett, Geo. Washing'n	36	Connecticut	Ass'r & Col'r	" "
Hunt, Benj. Thompson	33	Kentucky	Supt.S.F.Canal	" "
Hall, Albion Paris	29	Maine	Druggist	" "
Hernandez, R. Stephen	41	Florida	Stationer	" "
Hill, Whitman Hopper	30	Georgia	Clerk	" "
Hayes, Henry Brown	58	Vermont	Blacksmith	" "
Hendrix, William	47	Ohio	Farmer	" "
Hogan, Philip Barringer.	51	Indiana	Lime manufac'r	Diamond Springs T'p.
Hofmeister, Frederick	37	Germany	Hotel-keeper	Placerville Township.
Hill, William Johnson	39	Ohio	Farmer	Mud Springs "
Heisamann, Charles	47	Germany	Barber	Newtown.
Holmes, Elemuel Oliver	42	Kentucky	Miner	Placerville Township.
Holloway, W. McGeorge.	37	Indiana	Farmer	" "
Harms, Henry William	35	Germany	Barkeeper	Georgetown "
Hook, Geo. Washington	52	Kentucky		Placerville "
Hagan, Patrick	30	Ireland	Milkman	" "
Heusner, Conrad	33	Germany	Farmer	Mud Springs "
Huff, James Jacob	57	New York	"	" "
Hopkins, Griffith	37	Wales	Miner	Placerville "
Hendricks, Jesse King	38	Kentucky	Laborer	White Oak "
Holmes, Charles Burt	39	Ohio	Miner	Diamond Sp'gs "
Householder, Jonathan	36	Pennsylvania	"	Placerville "
Hertig, Gottleib	36	Switzerland	Farmer	Latrobe "
Hall, Daniel Tompkins	41	New York	Hotel-keeper	Shingle Springs.
Haggart, John D	61	New York	Farmer	Uniontown.
Hackler, John Pleasant	36	Tennessee	Miner	"
Hawson, Caldwell	41	New York	Farmer	"
Haggart, Daniel	33	New York	"	Coloma.
Hammond, Saml. Hobart	32	New York		
Hodgkin, John William	43	New York	Merchant	White Oak Township.
Huntington, Ithamar C	61	Vermont	Miner	Placerville.
Holmes, Irwin Isaac	48	Pennsylvania	"	"
Holmes, John	37	Vermont	Blacksmith	"
Hays, Cicero	28	Ohio	Clerk	"
House, George Henry	42	New York	Miner	" Township.
Haderle, John	32	Germany	"	Diamond Sp. Township
Huey, William Riley	31	Indiana	Hotel Keeper	" "
Henry, Thomas	62	Tennessee	Farmer	" "
Holcomb, Geo. Washing'n	38	Missouri	Miner	" "
Holmes, Jacob Pittinger	39	Ohio	Farmer	" "
Hanchett, Joseph Edward	21	Wisconsin	"	" "
Hubbard, William	50	New York		" "
Hufft, Philip Newton	48	Kentucky	Miner	" "
Holcomb, Horatio	56	Georgia	"	" "
Hagan, Peter	55	Ireland	Farmer	Placerville
Hanna, Davis	36	Delaware	Miner	Grizzly Flat.
Harvey, Obed	40	New York	Physician	Placerville.
Hood, Samuel	32	Nova Scotia	Engineer	"
Hollar, John Stevens	34	Indiana	Farmer	Indian Diggings.
Haas, James Charles	25	Bavaria	Miner	Pleasant Valley.

GREAT REGISTER, [H] EL DORADO COUNTY.

NAMES.	Age	Place of Nativity.	Occupation.	Local Residence.
Hardie, Angus McPherson	27	Scotland	Miner	Placerville.
Hunter, Geo. Washington	37	Indiana	Merchant	Greenwood Township.
Hardie, Oswald	31	Scotland	Miner	Placerville.
Heriot, William	41	Scotland	Merchant	White Oak Township.
Hardie, Thomas	40	Scotland	Farmer	Placerville.
Hart, William	52	Kentucky	Miner	Georgetown.
Hussey, James	30	N. Hampshire	"	"
Haddix, Jesse	33	Kentucky	"	"
Huber, Jacob	45	Pennsylvania	Farmer	" Township.
Handy, George	34	Ohio	Lumberman	" "
Holmes, Edward	24	Wisconsin	Miner	" "
Hosford, Martin	41	Ohio	"	" "
Hill, Brown	23	Ohio	Shoemaker	" "
Hyatt, Alexander Alvin	40	Connecticut	Banker	" "
Hart, Andrew Jackson	34	Virginia	Miner	" "
Handy, Philo	24	Ohio	Lumberman	" "
Hatfield, Wm. McKindrey	40	Ohio	Miner	Gold Hill.
Hunsucker, George	38	North Carolina	"	Kelsey Township.
Hunsucker, John	40	North Carolina	"	" "
Hale, William James	38	Kentucky	Rancher	" "
Herr, Abraham	60	Pennsylvania	Farmer	Coyoteville.
Hartman, James Smith	51	Pennsylvania	"	Spanish Creek.
Hill, Thomas	47	Kentucky	"	South Fork.
Humphreys, Geo. Wash'n	46	Virginia	"	Fair Play.
Howard, Thomas	33	Kentucky	Miner	Pilot Hill.
Hines, John	42	Maryland	"	Spanish Dry Diggings.
Hanson, Atwood James	42	Maine	"	Greenwood Township.
Horr, Geo. Washington	32	Massachusetts	"	" "
Harvey, Theodore Henry	30	New York	Blacksmith	" "
Hogg, John Baptist	48	Tennessee	Miner	Pilot Hill.
Hayes, Silas	64	Connecticut	Farmer	" "
Harris, William	52	Pennsylvania	"	Greenwood Township.
Holing, Anthony	29	Indiana	Miner	" "
Horine, Henry	35	Kentucky	Ferryman	" "
Harvey, And. William	39	Virginia	Miner	Duncan's Store.
Hulburd, Luther Tilden	44	New York	Saloon-keeper	Shingle Springs.
Hickman, Isaiah	50	Tennessee	Rancher	El Dorado.
Hankinson, Hen. Coursin	40	New Jersey	Laborer	Kelly Flat.
Heinz, Louis C. Francis	25	Kentucky	Clerk	Shingle Springs.
Hooning, Jacob	31	New York	Restaurant	" "
Hyneman, Samuel	33	Pennsylvania	Miner	El Dorado.
Higgins, Charles "T"	26	New York	"	" "
Hayes, James Crayton	31	Indiana	Livery Stable	Shingle Springs.
Hartless, Benj. Wyatt	37	Tennessee	Teamster	Diamond Springs Tp.
Hart, Sewell Page	54	N. Hampshire	Farmer	Shingle Springs.
Hutchinson, Geo. Wash.	61	Tennessee	Blacksmith	Missouri Flat.
Hoag, Philander Milton	36	New York	Miner	El Dorado.
Harper, John Randolph	38	Kentucky	Saloon Keeper	Latrobe.
Howe, Alphonso	33	Vermont	Laborer	Shingle Springs.
Hitchcock, Thomas	55	Ohio	Farmer	Latrobe.
Hunt, Edwin Rithburn	31	Vermont	Miner	El Dorado.
Hubbard, Chauncy	41	New York	"	Volcanoville.
Henry, George	66	Ireland	Carpenter	Diamond Springs Tp.
Hansen, Rasmus	44	Denmark	Constable	White Oak Township.
Heidrich, Jacob	44	Germany	Farmer	" "
Herber, Nicholas	49	Germany	Miner	Diamond Springs Tp.
Hinman, Marquis Desalvo	49	New York	Physician	Mud Springs "
Hewett, Moses Dakin	34	Maine	Farmer	Diamond Springs "
Harden, John Barten	43	Indiana	Wheelwright	Georgetown "
Horton, Stephen Wesley	36	Georgia	Miner	" "
Hoffmaster, Mathew	39	Denmark	"	Kelsey "
Horin, Timothy	31	Ireland	Saddler	Mud Springs "
Henley, Richard	38	Ireland	Miner	Kelsey "

NAME.	Age	Place of Nativity.	Occupation.	Local Residence.
Hamilton, Henry Sibley	46	England	Butcher	Georgetown Township.
Hoffman, Gustave	36	Saxony	Hotel keeper	" "
Hebrew, James	45	Ireland	Miner	" "
Howard, Burrill Chase	53	Vermont	"	" "
Houston, Charles Webster	40	Massachusetts	"	" "
Healey, Michael	32	Great Britain	"	" "
Hurley, Timothy	46	Ireland	"	Greenwood Township.
Hammel, Benedict	43	Wurtemburg	"	" "
Hussi, Laurence	38	Bavaria	"	" "
Hanle, Leo Remigus	39	Germany	"	" "
Hawkins, Patrick	37	Ireland	Farmer	Salmon Falls "
Hawkins, John	38	Ireland	"	" " "
Hamilton, Thomas	41	Scotland	Miner	Greenwood "
Harney, Charles	36	Great Britain	Blacksmith	Coloma "
Hughes, Matthew	44	Ireland	Miner	" "
Howard, Matthew	36	England	"	White Oak "
Hopwood, Frank. Marion	34	Virginia	"	Salmon Falls "
Hensel, John	52	Prussia	"	White Oak "
Hart, Powell	42	Holland	Farmer	Salmon Falls "
Hoover, John Alexander	27	Ohio	"	" " "
Harper, Matthew	30	England	Miner	Mud Springs "
Henley, Andrew	32	Wurtemburg	Blacksmith	" " "
Helton, John	54	Tennessee	Wood chopper	" " "
Hitchcock, Elmore	28	Ohio	Farmer	" " "
Holdridge, Lewis	55	New York	"	White Oak "
Heinz, Conrad	56	Germany	Saloon keeper	Mud Springs "
Henley, Patrick	29	Great Britain	Farmer	" " "
Hughes, William Carson	41	Canada	Painter	" " "
Holdridge, Daniel Hate	25	Illinois	Farmer	White Oak "
Higgins, Dennis	38	Ireland	"	Mud Springs "
Holt, Edwin	41	Great Britain	Toll keeper	Mountain "
Holcomb, Joseph	33	Missouri	Miner	" "
Hufnagel, Frederick Wm	44	Prussia	"	Cosumnes "
Hartman, Nicholas	52	France	"	" "
Hartman, George	45	France	"	" "
Howk, Adam	33	Baden	"	" "
Harleby, Morris	36	Ireland	"	" "
Herman, Michael	44	Bavaria	"	" "
Heberle, Adam	37	Germany	"	" "
Hartley, Henry James	37	Great Britain	"	Placerville "
Harris, Morris	50	Prussia	Trader	Mud Springs "
Harvey, John Henry	40	Great Britain	Miner	" " "
Hickey, Michael	27	Ireland	Laborer	" " "
Hartmayer, Louis	37	Wurtemburg	Miner	" " "
Harris, Abraham	33	Russia	Merchant	" " "
Hunt, William	60	Ireland	Miner	" " "
Hickey, Patrick	38	Ireland	"	Diamond Sp'gs "
Haas, John	36	France	"	" " "
Harmes, Christopher	37	Hanover	Hotel keeper	" " "
Harper, Elliott	30	Ireland	Laborer	Placerville "
Hinkle, Solomon	68	South Carolina	Farmer	" "
Heublein, Lorenzo	39	Germany	Saddler	Shingle Sp'gs "
Henderson, Jesse Gray	38	Georgia	Miner	Placerville "
Hartman, John	55	Germany	Laborer	" "
Harkness, George	46	Germany	"	" "
Hartman, John	29	New York	Miner	" "
Huber, Joseph	22	Germany	Blacksmith	Coloma "
Hixon, Thomas Lasy	56	Virginia	"	Placerville.
Hoyt, William Wallace	24	Canada	Farmer	Diamond Springs Tp
Hogan, Charles	21	Iowa	Cooper	Placerville "
Hayes, William	34	Ireland	Miner	Shingle Springs.
Hab, Henry	44	France	Physician	Placerville "
Hiller, William Richard	56	Bavaria	Farmer	Gold Hill "

NAME.	Age	Place of Nativity.	Occupation.	Local Residence.
Heindel, Daniel	35	Ohio	Miner	Georgetown Township.
Haas, Frederick Reder	37	New York	"	" "
Harkness, Edson	33	Ohio	Farmer	" "
Hotchkiss, William Henry	46	Vermont	Teamster	" "
Hinkley, Thomas Spear	30	Maine	Miner	" "
Haber, Jacob	46	Pennsylvania	Farmer	" "
Harkness, Roderick Due	41	Ohio	"	" "
Hall, John Francis	42	Missouri	Miner	Diamond Springs T'p.
Hodges, John Bailey	46	Tennessee	"	" " "
Haskins, Erastus Moore	60	New York	Merchant	" " "
Howard, William Bailey	49	Kentucky	Farmer	Gold Hill.
Hutcheson, Thomas	67	North Carolina	"	Coloma.
Higgins, Jeremiah	42	Maine	"	Uniontown.
Henderson, I. Hendrick	37	Indiana	Miner	Cold Springs.
Heatt, Alfred	47	Virginia	Mason	Nashville.
Harvey, Henry Clay	35	Virginia	Miner	"
Henniger, Thos. Jefferson	36	Virginia	Carpenter	El Dorado.
Hazelton, Aaron Carter	44	New York	Milling	Latrobe.
Hart, Charles Edward	33	New York	Gen'l business.	El Dorado.
Hart, Oliver Perry	40	Tennessee	Miner	Nashville.
Ham, Ephram	34	New York	Carpenter	El Dorado.
Hanna, Franklin	46	Virginia	Teamster	Shingle Springs.
Harmer, James Leander	35	Virginia	Miner	Cosumnes Township.
Henson, William Farmer	41	Kentucky	"	" "
Harrold, Charles	63	N. Hampshire	"	White Oak "
Harding, William	49	Connecticut	"	Kelsey "
Herrick, Lorenzo	42	New York	"	" "
Hoffman, William	38	Pennsylvania	"	" "
Honey, Joseph Hemphill	51	N. Hampshire	Farmer	Placerville "
Henderson, Sam'l Clinton	40	Ohio	Miner	" "
Hill, William Harvey	26	Illinois	Teamster	" "
Holmes, Gordon Vernon	42	South Carolina	Miner	Mountain "
Heckert, Henry	33	Pennsylvania	Carpenter	" "
Hakenoller, Henry	41	Hanover	Farmer	Kelsey "
Holmes, Elisha	64	Massachusetts	Miner	Georgetown "
Hanson, William	29	Ohio	"	" "
Hanson, Sanford	41	Ohio	"	" "
Hudson, James	49	Virginia	"	" "
Haydon, George Warren	46	Vermont	"	" "
Hall, William	42	Ohio	"	" "
Harris, Eliphalet Ward	39	Connecticut	Shoemaker	Diamond Springs T'p.
Holmes, Russell Bar. Rin.	24	Missouri	Miner	" "
Hancock, Jas. Anderson	36	Tennessee	"	Placerville "
Houghton, Milo	28	Vermont	Laborer	"
Hoyt, Henry	40	New York	Miner	Placerville Township.
Hicks, John	54	Great Britain	Teamster	" "
Hand, Joseph	33	Indiana	Miner	" "
Hueser, William	57	Prussia	Stone mason	Georgetown "
Beldman, Frederick Wm.	38	Germany	Merchant	Brownsville.
Halls, Isaac	39	England	Miner	Georgetown Township.
Henke, William	38	Prussia	"	Diamond Springs T'p.
Hathaway, Edmund Val.	27	Massachusetts	Gardener	Mud Springs "
Hooker, Van Buren	34	Virginia	Miner	Placerville "
Holmes, Zephniar	40	Illinois	"	" "
Hanlon, Michael	32	Ireland	Farmer	Mountain "
Hanley, Patrick Richard	39	Ireland	Miner	Mud Springs "
Hoover, William Harrison	26	Indiana	"	Georgetown "
Hussey, George Varney	43	N. Hampshire	Carpenter	" "
Hawley, Asa Hershel	53	Vermont	Dairyman	Lake Valley Township.
Hughes, Elbert Kelsey	27	Missouri	Laborer	" " "
Harvey, Charles Wesley	34	New York	Hotel Keeper	" " "
Hayden, Charles Barber	66	Maine	Miner	Salmon Falls "
Hoffman, Chauncey Basset	36	New York	"	" " "

NAME.	Age	Place of Nativity.	Occupation.	Local Residence.
Horton, Otis Hiram	64	Massachusetts	Seaman	Coloma Township.
Henry, Joseph	40	Tennessee	Miner	Greenwood.
Hewey, Thomas	63	Tennessee	Farmer	Grizzly Flat.
Hughes, Peter Pence	50	Ohio	Miner	Cosumnes Township.
Hammill, Bradford	44	New York	Farmer	El Dorado.
Hatch, James Davron	26	New York	Stage Driver	"
Hartzough, David Beard	61	Michigan	Teamster	"
Hunt, Arthur Livermore	27	Maine	Farmer	"
Hill, Samuel	44	Ohio	Miner	"
House, Robert	84	New York	"	"
Hunt, Edwin Rithburne	31	Vermont	"	"
Hitchcock, Aaron Corey	33	Ohio	Farmer	Latrobe.
Hitchcock, Isaac Nathan	34	Ohio	"	"
Hills, Bolivar	40	Indiana	Miner	Shingle Springs.
Hills, Bowman Gelkey	38	Indiana	"	" "
Hills, John	67	Kentucky	"	" "
Hastings, James Hannum	...	Ohio	Laborer	Latrobe.
Hunt, Warren	57	Connecticut	"	King's Store.
Harlick, Absolem	41	Pennsylvania	Miner	Latrobe.
Hensler, John Daniel	44	Germany	Copper-smith	Georgetown Township.
Hill, George	45	Ireland	Miner	Greenwood "
Holden, Reuben	21	New York	"	White Oak "
Hicks, Gilbert	24	Wisconsin	Teamster	Placerville "
Hewitt, Oken Clay	29	Virginia	Toll Keeper	" "
Hungerford, Morgan	48	New York	Millwright	Grizzly Flat.
Hayden, James	30	Illinois	Miner	Lake Valley Township.
Hitchens, John, Jr	23	Australia	"	Georgetown "

I

NAME.	Age	Place of Nativity.	Occupation.	Local Residence.
Ingham, George Henry	42	New York	Lawyer	Coloma Township.
Immner, Joseph	34	Baden	Miner	" "
Immner, August	31	Baden	Farmer	" "
Ingham, Samuel Saltus	39	New York	Lumberman	Georgetown "
Irwin, Charles Fitzgerald	38	New York	Attor'y at Law	Placerville "
Irons, Elijah	46	Ohio	Miner	Kelsey "
Irish, Joseph	32	Maine	Teamster	Shingle Springs.
Inness, Joseph Mixsill	38	Pennsylvania	"	" "
Isbell, Philo Judson	43	Connecticut	Farmer	Georgetown Township.
Irvine, John Easley	60	Virginia	"	White Oak "
Ilsohm, John Fred. David	37	Hamburg	Hotel-keeper	Diamond Springs Tp.
Irvine, James Wethers	45	Alabama	Laborer	El Dorado.
Isinger, John Andrew	34	Ohio	Jeweler	Pilot Hill.
Ingersoll, Hiram	37	Ohio	Teamster	Sly Park.

J

NAME.	Age	Place of Nativity.	Occupation.	Local Residence.
Johnson, James	55	Kentucky	Lawyer	Placerville Township.
Johnson, Geo. Washingt'n	64	Massachusetts	Farmer	White Oak "
Jones, Abriam	35	Tennessee	Teamster	" "
Jackson, Charles Pringle	46	New York	Rancher	El Dorado.
Jones, William Henry	28	Ohio	Constable	Coloma Township.
Jones, Edwin Ruthrin	34	Michigan	Miner	Placerville "
Jamison, John	54	Scotland	"	" "
Jones, Evans Poulteny	43	Wales	"	" "
Jewell, Godfrey	28	England	Merchant	" "
Jones, Charles	32	Maine	Miner	Pilot Hill.
Jess, William Francis	33	Maryland	Carpenter	Placerville Township.
Jones, William	47	New York	Lumberman	" "
Johns, David Don	40	Ohio	Liquor Merc'ht	" "
Johnson, John Cahoun	44	Ohio	Farmer	" "
Jones, Edward Russell	47	Vermont	Miner	" "
Johnson, Charles John	45	Sweden	Farmer	Coloma.

NAME.	Age	Place of Nativity.	Occupation.	Local Residence.
Johnson, Benjamin	62	Ohio	Farmer	Placerville Township.
Jennings, John	56	Ireland	Shoemaker	" "
Jackson, Giles Andrew	39	Ohio	Carpenter	" "
Jamison, William	24	Scotland	Farmer	" "
Johnson, James	39	England	"	" "
Jessup, Emerson	28	Massachusetts	Agent	" "
Jacobson, Rudolph	36	Denmark	Hotel-keeper	Smith's Flat.
Johnson, William	33	Illinois	Miner	Fair Play.
James, John Calvin	51	England	Engineer	Placerville.
Jolly, Francis Marion	43	Indiana	Farmer	El Dorado.
Jopling, Launcelot	56	England	Miner	Placerville Township.
Jerrett, Daniel	36	New York	Livery	Georgetown "
Jamad, Charles	36	New York	Miner	" "
Jabine, William	46	Maryland	"	Kelsey "
Jenkerson, Aug. Henry	28	Missouri	"	Brownsville.
James, John	42	Kentucky	"	Fair Play.
Jackson, Gil. Ford. Dolsen	48	New York	"	Pilot Hill.
Jones, Thomas	48	Pennsylvania	"	" "
Jones, Conrad	52	Pennsylvania	Tailor	" "
Jack, Thomas Ely	28	Ohio	Teamster	Shingle Springs.
Jones, James Buvris	30	Delaware	Miner	"
Jackson, Julius Dunham	37	New York	Book-keeper	El Dorado.
James, Alfred	39	Ohio	Miner	Kelsey.
Johnson, James	52	England	Laborer	Placerville.
Johnson, John	48	England	Miner	White Oak Township.
Jackson, Isaac Priestly	38	North Carolina	Merchant	Georgetown "
Johnston, Barnard	38	Great Britain	Miner	Kelsey "
Jacobs, Abiezer-Boldy	41	Upper Canada	"	Georgetown "
Jerguson, N. Chas. Martin	42	Denmark	"	Greenwood "
Jenkins, John Ewing	43	Scotland	"	Salmon Falls "
Jeffers, Samuel	64	New York	Laborer	Mud Springs "
Jacobs, Solomon	35	Russia	Merchant	Georgetown "
Johnston, William	30	Ireland	Miner	Kelsey "
Johnson, Benjamin	52	Ohio	Farmer	Placerville "
Johnson, Uriah	36	Pennsylvania	Semeter	" "
Jurgens, Jasper	43	England	Quartz Miner	White Oak "
Jurgens, Berrend	41	Hanover	Farmer	Mud Springs "
Jackson, Thomas	25	Scotland	Miner	Coloma "
Jones, Thomas Jefferson	40	Tennessee	Clerk	Placerville "
Johnson, Wm. Heuston	35	Tennessee	Farmer	Georgetown "
Jacott, David	27	Michigan	Carpenter	" "
Johnson, Wm. Harrison	25	New York	Farmer	Diamond Sp. "
James, Walter	30	Ohio	"	Kelsey "
Jordan, Moses	30	S. Carolina	Miner	Uniontown.
Jones, John	55	Pennsylvania	Farmer	Coloma Township.
Johns, Benj. Franklin	35	Tennesseee	Miner	El Dorado.
Jamison, Jesse Ewing	39	Kentucky	"	" "
James, Henry Jefferson	38	Kentucky	"	Indian Diggings.
Jackson, Lindsey Marshall	40	Missouri	Farmer	White Oak Township.
Jewell, Abraham Day	29	New York	"	" "
Jordan, John Edward	38	Maine	Miner	Kelsey "
Jewell, Edwin Lewis	38	Massachusetts	"	" "
Jenks, Franklin Adelbert	25	New York	"	Greenwood "
Jewett, Henry Marsh	36	Massachusetts	Painter	Placerville "
Joiner, Benjamin	31	South Carolina	Miner	Grizzly Flat.
Jones, Henry Samuel	40	New York	"	Mud Springs Township.
Jacobson, Alexander	36	Denmark	"	Coloma "
Jordan, Joshua	37	Maine	"	White Oak "
Jaeger, George Francis	26	Germany	"	Placerville "
Jacobson, John	28	Denmark	"	White Oak "
Jeffreys, Gideon	44	Great Britain	"	Placerville "
Jenkinson, Robert	46	Ireland	Farmer	" "
Jacobson, Hans	39	Sweden	"	" "

NAME.	Age	Place of Nativity.	Occupation.	Local Residence.
Jackson, Geo. Longley	27	Ireland	Miner	Placerville Township.
Jones, James Edward	47	Kentucky	"	Georgetown "
Johnson, Lemuel	47	Tennessee	Laborer	Lake Valley "
Jones, Edwin Augustus	45	Georgia	Carpenter	Salmon Falls "
Jacobs, Geo. Washington	35	New York	Farmer	Uniontown.
Jewell, Justice Brown	53	New York	Miner	Placerville Township.
Jones, Charles Jackson	43	Georgia	Farmer	" "
Jones, Thomas	67	Maryland	Miner	Latrobe.
Johnson, Thomas Stewart	37	New York	Lawyer	Placerville Township.
Johnson, Uriah Zefend	35	Pennsylvania	Laborer	" "
Johnson, William	44	Sweeden	Farmer	White Oak "

K

NAME.	Age	Place of Nativity.	Occupation.	Local Residence.
Kinseley, Peter	30	New Jersey	Miner	White Oak Township.
Kimball, Thos. Jefferson	40	Maine	Farmer	" " "
Kies, George Orville	36	New York	Printer	Placerville.
Kilmer, Cornelius	54	New York	"	" "
Kugler, Christian Karl	35	Wurtemburg	Miner	White Oak "
Knighton, John	52	England	"	" " "
Kolzeman, Edward	38	Germany	None	Placerville "
Kunkler, John Ernest	28	Switzerland	Physician	" "
Kramp, William Antone	37	Nassau	Farmer	Diamond Sp'gs "
Kirchner, George	48	Bavaria	"	Pilot Hill.
Keller, John Frederick	40	Bavaria	Brewer	Diamond Sp'gs "
Kane, Patrick	35	Ireland	Miner	Coloma "
Keegan, Edward	50	Ireland	Farmer	Placerville "
Kerns, Thomas Jefferson	29	Illinois	Miner	Mountain "
Keding, Heneuck	40	Germany	Shoemaker	Placerville "
Krahner, William	44	Germany	Farmer	" "
Kepheart, George	35	Pennsylvania	"	Kelsey "
Kone, James	34	Great Britain	Ditch Agent	Coloma "
Kelley, Michael	40	Ireland	Miner	Placerville "
King, George Washington	38	New York	"	" "
Kaiser, Jacob	52	Germany	"	" "
Kramp, Phillip	32	Germany	"	Diamond Sp'gs "
Koebler, Adolph	35	Germany	Ditch Agent	Coloma.
Kidd, Moses	49	Illinois	Farmer	Placerville "
Kendricks, Albert	33	New York	Hotel Clerk	" "
Knox, Gilbert Worthy	36	Connecticut	Miner	" "
Kerr, John W	34	Virginia	Carpenter	Sportsman Hall.
Kinney, Ephraim Lampson	45	Maine	"	Placerville "
King, Charles Melzar	53	Vermont	Feed stable k'p'r	" "
Kane, John	50	Ireland	Laborer	" "
Kischner, Michael	41	Bavaria	Miner	Coloma "
Kent, Albert Nelson	24	Massachusetts	Clerk	Placerville "
Konze, Dominicus	60	Prussia	Farmer	" "
Kennedy, Joseph	40	Ireland	"	" "
Kipp, John Louis	35	Prussia	Miner	White Oak "
Kirkpatrick, John	27	Illinois	"	Cold Springs.
Kennedy, Andrew Jackson	36	New York	Assessor	Coloma "
Killough, John Wesley	37	Indiana	Miner	" "
Kennedy, Henry	55	Ireland	"	Kelsey "
Kirk, John	52	Pennsylvania	Contractor	Placerville "
Kuckenmeister, Benedict	39	Germany	Watchmaker	El Dorado.
Kemp, William	34	New York	Cooper	Placerville "
Knight, Thomas Scott	39	Vermont	Farmer	Diamond Sp'gs "
Kidder, John Flint	36	New York	Civil Engineer	Shingle Sp'gs.
Knowlton, Egb't Brigham	29	New York	Miner	Smith's Flat.
Knox, Shannon	52	Pennsylvania	Carpenter	Georgetown.
Keller, Alexander	21	Indiana	Farmer	"
Knox, Milo Douglass	27	Pennsylvania	Miner	"
Klipstein, James	45	Virginia	"	"

NAMES.	Age	Place of Nativity.	Occupation.	Local Residence.
Keefer, Jesse Rhodes	23	Ohio	Toll-keeper	Lake Valley Township.
Kimball, John	31	Pennsylvania	Hostler	" " "
Kent, Sherman	42	New York	Farmer	" " "
Kinsey, John Edgar	29	New York	Ferryman	Salmon Falls "
Kelsey, Jonathan	38	Connecticut	Miner	Kelsey "
Kingsley, James Foreman	34	Pennsylvania	Merchant	Diamond Springs T'p.
Kelsea, Moses Hubbard	40	N. Hampshire	Miner	Longtown "
Kinney, William	50	Kentucky	Teamster	Shingle Springs.
Kern, Andrew	38	Germany	Butcher	Greenwood Township.
King, Johnson	47	Tennessee	Miner	Georgetown "
Keegan, Simon	35	Ireland	Merchant	Diamond Springs "
Kesselring, Adam	43	Germany	Farmer	Coloma "
Kelley, Patrick	42	Ireland	Miner	Kelsey "
Knoesel, Chas. Henry L	37	Hanover	Blacksmith	" "
Konocke, George	50	Hanover	Miner	" "
Krauzfeldt, Christian	44	Holstein	Farmer	Georgetown "
Karbstine, Charles	42	Prussia	Butcher	" "
Keefer, William McClay	51	Pennsylvania	Farmer	" "
Knowles, William George	50	England	Butcher	" "
Knudeson, Hans Moller	51	Denmark	Miner	Greenwood "
Klumb, Jacob	44	Prussia	"	" "
Koepecke, Jno. Chas. F	56	Prussia	Farmer	Coloma "
Keefer, John Walton	34	Pennsylvania	"	White Oak "
Kies, James Henry	39	South Carolina	Stage Driver	Mud Springs "
Keegan, James	54	Ireland	Gardener	White Oak "
Killpatrick, D. McCibbin	43	Ohio	Merchant	Georgetown "
Knox, William	59	Ohio	Carpenter	Mountain "
Kyne, James	44	Ireland	Miner	" "
Keane, Patrick	40	Great Britain	Farmer	Cosumnes "
Kollock, Mathew Henry	33	Virginia	Physician	" "
Kelzow, John	37	Germany	Miner	" "
Kellen, John	29	Germany	"	" "
Korner, Henry	29	Saxony	"	Diamond Springs "
Kline, Martin	34	Germany	"	Placerville "
Koock, John Henry	59	Germany	"	Coloma "
Keeber, Deedrich	49	Hanover	"	Mud Springs "
Klotz, Joseph Anthony	40	Baden	Farmer	" " "
Kane, James	58	Ireland	Clerk	" " "
Krummel, John	54	Germany	Miner	Diamond Springs "
Keene, Alson	40	Maine	Carpenter	Placerville "
Koch, Bartel	38	Baden	Hotel-keeper	Diamond Springs "
Koch, Augustus	26	Baden	Butcher	" " "
Knighton, David Jackson	27	England	Miner	" " "
Kleinhammer, Chris. F	27	Denmark	"	Kelsey "
Kinnenmouth, Andrew	50	Scotland	Farmer	Georgetown "
Kinzel, John	48	Austria	Trader	Mud Springs "
Klieber, George	31	Bavaria	Miner	Coloma "
Kerbley, Michael Henry	27	Germany	Laborer	Latrobe "
Koletzke, August	30	Prussia	Miner	Mud Springs "
King, Joel Charles	54	North Carolina	"	Georgetown "
Keller, Anthony Hends'n	71	North Carolina	Farmer	" "
Kane, Dennis	51	New York	Cook	Diamond Springs "
Kerrigan, Thomas	39	Pennsylvania	Miner	" " "
Kelley, Alexander	37	New York	"	El Dorado.
Kinsely, Jacob	36	Ohio	Farmer	"
Knott, Jonathan	57	Maryland	Laborer	King's Store.
King, Weithers	55	Kentucky	Hotel-keeper	El Dorado.
Knowlton, John Winslow	47	Maine	Millwright	"
Kyburg, Samuel Elliott	25	Wisconsin	Farmer	White Oak Township.
Keefer, Joseph	37	Pennsylvania	"	" " "
Kenyon, Henry Peter	50	New York	Laborer	" " "
Karriater, Simon	34	Pennsylvania	Miner	" " "
Kern, John	28	Ohio	"	Placerville "

NAME.	Age	Place of Nativity.	Occupation.	Local Residence.
Kyser, James	32	Michigan	Miner	Placerville Township.
Kerns, Thomas Jefferson	29	Illinois	"	Mountain "
King, Elijah	39	Indiana	"	" "
King, Philip	33	Ohio	"	Placerville "
Kelley, Harvey	39	South Carolina	"	Georgetown "
Kimerer, Michael	35	Ohio	Farmer	Sly Park.
Kneeland, Hector Pryam	61	New York	Lumberman	"
Kelley, Simpson Daney	38	Virginia	Teamster	"
Knight, John	30	England	Miner	Georgetown Township.
Kloepfer, Louis	39	Bavaria	Farmer	Coloma "
Kind, Jonas	23	Bohemia	Merchant	Georgetown "
Kimball, Thos. Laurence	30	New York	Miner	" "
Kay, Isaac Newton	42	Ohio	Toll Collector	Lake Valley "
Kent, Sherman	44	New York	Dairyman	" "
Kennedy, Alfred Edward	36	New York	Carpenter	Coloma. "
Keyser, William D	38	Pennsylvania	Farmer	Placerville "
Kemp, John	43	Pennsylvania	Machinist	" "
Kinkade, Logan	29	Virginia	Miner	Grizzly Flat.
Kelley, Robert Paul	36	New York	"	El Dorado.
Kertle, Martin Lafayette	30	Georgia	Laborer	Latrobe.
Kay, George Smith	48	Scotland	Farmer	Georgetown Township.
Kirkeep, Val. Simpson	36	England	Miner	Cosumnes "

L

NAME.	Age	Place of Nativity.	Occupation.	Local Residence.
Lockwood, Wm. Rufus	57	New York	Miner	White Oak Township.
Long, Felix Decatur	38	Pennsylvania	Saloon-keeper	" "
Litton, Arthur	35	Illinois	Farmer	" "
Laaker, Henry	32	Prussia	Laborer	Placerville "
Lowry, Albert Jay	36	Ohio	Postmaster	" "
Lovless, Philip J	35	Georgia	Miner	White Oak "
Lumbard, Charles	43	Massachusetts	Clerk	Placerville "
Lee, Albert Thomas	36	Tennessee	Saloon-keeper	" "
Lamb, John Shugarts	52	Pennsylvania	Miner	" "
Lutter, Antone	44	Prussia	Farmer	Coloma "
Lind, Mathew	40	Pennsylvania	House-joiner	Diamond Sp. "
Lohry, Adam	46	Germany	Merchant	Uniontown.
Lewis, John Hopkins	49	Kentucky	Miner	Placerville Township,
Lewis, Granville Thomas	48	Kentucky	"	" "
Leachman, Austin Taylor	36	Kentucky	Farmer	Salmon Falls "
Libby, John Watson	37	Massachusetts	Engineer	Placerville "
Lemon, Samuel	41	Pennsylvania	Miner	" "
Lacy, William	41	Scotland	Stable-keeper	" "
Leslie, Andrew	50	Ireland	Miner	" "
Leslie, Joseph	62	Ireland	"	" "
Lewellin, Saml. Septimus	42	England	"	White Oak "
Linder, Moses Norton	27	Illinois	"	Placerville "
Lampman, Jacob	39	New York	Teamster	" "
Lyon, Jacob	49	Kentucky	Farmer	" "
Laughlin, Benj. Marion	37	Illinois	Constable	" "
Lowell, William Henry	35	Maryland	Harness-maker	" "
Leon, George Taylor	34	Rhode Island	Miner	" "
Lemon, Calvin	30	Pennsylvania	"	" "
Larned, Wellington	33	New York	Teamster	" "
Leslie, James	33	Pennsylvania	"	" "
Leach, David Walter	28	Maine	Lumberman	Pleasant Valley.
Lewis, William	66	Massachusetts	Farmer	Placerville Township.
Lapham, Henry Dearborn	45	Rhode Island	"	" "
Limpinsel, Frederick	45	Prussia	Miner	Cold Springs.
Larkin, Jared Lockwood	35	New York	Farmer	Diamond Sp. Township.
Ludinghouse, Frederick	30	Prussia	Wagon Maker	Placerville "
Lyman, Patrick Henry	37	Ireland	Farmer	White Oak "
Lawson, Samuel	42	Sweden	Miner	Kelsey "

NAMES.	Age	Place of Nativity.	Occupation.	Local Residence.
Larson, Jens	40	Denmark	Miner	Greenwood Township.
Lawyer, John Jay	47	New York	Merchant	American Flat.
Lewis, George	34	Maine	Miner	Cold Springs.
Loofbourrow, D. Thomas	37	Ohio	Merchant	" "
Lowe, Joseph P.	33	Ohio	Artist	Coloma.
Lapham, Darius	31	Michigan	Teamster	Placerville Township.
Larkin, Henry	40	New York	Farmer	Diamond Springs Tp.
Lewis, Hugh	43	England	Miner	Diamond Springs Tp.
Lambert, Thomas	51	England	Farmer	Mud Springs Township.
Linck, Henry	42	Germany	Baker	Greenwood "
Lape, John Thomas	51	New York	Miner	Salmon Falls "
Lasky, Abraham Marks	46	Russia	Merchant	El Dorado.
Lazinsky, Himan	22	Austria	Miner	Greenwood Township.
Lorton, Samuel Smith	36	Illinois	Livery	Georgetown "
Lyman, Walter Harris	50	Vermont	Miner	" "
Lawrence, Nathaniel	40	Massachusetts	"	Kelsey "
Little, William Adams	62	Pennsylvania	"	" "
Lusk, Charles Wesley	43	New York	"	" "
Long, Solomon Alexander	40	Virginia	Water Agent	Diamond Springs T'p.
Lander, George	40	New York	Miner	Diamond Springs Tp.
Locke, Isaac Stanwood	42	Maine	"	Indian Diggings.
Lamb, Thomas Robinson	29	Pennsylvania	"	" "
Lupton, Jos. Constantine	32	Missouri	"	Brownsville.
Livingston, Spence	49	New York	Physician	Pilot Hill.
Lovejoy, Lorriston Hale	47	Maine	Farmer	" "
Lee, Reuben Munson	48	Connecticut	Miner	Spanish Dry Diggings.
Lamphere, Judsen	34	New York	Teamster	Shingle Springs.
Land, William "C."	30	Texas	Livery	" "
Lillebridge, D. Markham	46	Ohio	Laborer	El Dorado.
Leonard, John Peter	32	Connecticut	"	Shingle Springs.
Laville, Alexander	28	Illinois	"	" "
Laverty, Melvin	43	New York	Miner	Placerville Township.
Lowman, John Clark	43	Ohio	"	" "
Long, Thomas	30	England	Farmer	Kelsey "
Lippe, Schaneburge	39	Germany	Miner	Mud Springs "
Lewis, Thomas Fielding	38	Kentucky	Constable	Georgetown "
Labaree, Seth	30	Missouri	Miner	Kelsey "
Lavanino, Louis	25	Italy	"	Diamond Springs Tp.
Lawlor, James	55	Great Britain	"	Kelsey "
Largerson, Frederick	36	Denmark	"	" "
Laumann, Jonn. Nichoby	37	Norway	"	" "
Lalmar, Dominique	43	Germany	"	Georgetown "
Leslie, Alexander	55	North Carolina	"	Greenwood "
Lamb, Geo. Washington	37	Missouri	"	" "
Lazansky, Bernhard	28	Bohemia	"	White Oak "
Lahr, Pierre	42	Luxemburg	"	" "
Leahy, Daniel	39	Great Britain	"	" "
Lloyd, Charles	45	Wales	Store-keeper	Salmon Falls "
Lamb, Carrington Billings	48	Connecticut	Blacksmith	" "
Lane, Samuel Augustus	37	Maine	Miner	Mud Springs "
Lane, Richard	41	Virginia	Laborer	" "
Linnemann, Benjamin	39	Hanover	Blacksmith	" "
Linville, William Presley	35	Mississippi	Farmer	" "
Land, John	33	Mississippi	Stable-keeper	" "
Lepley, Phillips	30	Ohio	Miner	Mountain "
Lokump, Henry	45	Prussia	"	Cosumnes "
Lentz, Charles	47	Wirtemburg	"	" "
Lawrence, John Sinclair	30	Great Britain	Farmer	Greenwood "
Laiderich, John James	30	France	Miner	Georgetown "
Leutzinger, Henry	37	Switzerland	Brewer	Coloma "
Levy, Joseph	45	Austria	Merchant	Diamond Springs Tp.
Lighthall, William	44	New York	Carpenter	Placerville "
Lower, William	41	Ohio	Cook	

NAME.	Age	Place of Nativity.	Occupation.	Local Residence.
Lewis, Henry	45	Russia	Merchant	Placerville Township.
Leneve, James Perry	33	Indiana	Miner	" "
Lachsman, Baptist	50	Italy	Laborer	Diamond Sp'gs "
Lepetit, Louis	47	Saxony	Lumberman	" " "
Lerch, Peter	29	Pennsylvania	Miner	Spanish Dry Diggings.
Lyford, John	63	N. Hampshire	Farmer	Placerville Township.
Lourin, Louis	76	Missouri	Miner	" "
Lombardi, Giavani	31	Italy	Gardener	" "
Lambert, Dan	23	Michigan	Farmer	Mud Springs "
Lockard, James Madison	43	Ohio	"	Placerville "
Lehr, Daniel	36	Ohio	Miner	" "
Lane, William Henry	35	Vermont	Tinner	Georgetown "
Larlat, Louis Erastus	52	Massachusetts	Miner	" "
Lee, Alexander Thompson	36	Pennsylvania	Teamster	" "
La Fourrette, Aaron Ogd.	35	New York	Farmer	Diamond Sp'gs "
Lynch, John Hollis	43	Pennsylvania	"	" " "
Lear, Henry Figens	36	Missouri	Miner	" " "
Leach, William Brown	43	Illinois	Saloon keeper	Nashville.
Lambert, Dan	22	Michigan	Laborer	Shingle Springs.
Larrison, David	34	New York	Farmer	Latrobe.
Luce, Andrew Jackson	34	Maine	Miner	Nashville.
Lay, Ephraim Anderson	51	SouthCarolina	"	Brownsville.
Little, Jackson	33	Indiana	"	"
Lea, Francis Caswell	29	Tennessee	"	Indian Diggings.
Loveless, Seth	40	Ohio	Farmer	" "
Lomas, Samuel	53	Pennsylvania	Millwright	Cosumnes Township.
Lyons, William Henry	32	Illinois	Farmer	Lake Valley "
Lowery, Geo. Washington	35	Ohio	Miner	White Oak "
Larkin, Sylvester	26	Iowa	Laborer	Lake Valley "
Lane, Marshall Bolin	49	Tennessee	Farmer	Salmon Falls "
Layne, William Thomas	25	Tennessee	Miner	" " "
Lucas, Devillier	33	New York	Teamster	Placerville "
Love, Frank	21	Maine	Shingle maker	" "
Leifreid, Charles Henry	30	Pennsylvania	Harness maker	" "
Love, Louis Oliver	46	New York	Farmer	" "
Lee, Thomas	23	Wisconsin	Miner	Mountain "
Laflar, Geo. Washington	32	Ohio	"	" "
Lowry, Thomas Helms	50	Kentucky	"	" "
Longley, Harrison	39	Maine	"	" "
Lembert, Peter	36	New York	"	White Oak "
Lee, Henry Clay	36	Indiana	Farmer	Mud Springs "
List, James Harvey	34	Indiana	Miner	Georgetown "
Loomis, Salmon Hanm	28	Ohio	Marble worker	" "
Logan, Sampson Armst'g	42	Pennsylvania	Miner	" "
Lyon, Joseph	25	Indiana	"	Placerville "
Lucke, John	38	Prussia	"	White Oak "
Little, Hiram	42	Ohio	Laborer	Diamond Sp'gs "
Landers, Henry	34	Bavaria	Cook	" " "
Lusinke, Panto	35	France	Merchant	Georgetown "
Leveronia, Stefano	35	Italy	Miner	Diamond Sp'gs "
Leik, Wendel	36	Prussia	Farmer	Salmon Falls "
Lincln, Benjamin	42	Massachusetts	Miner	Halfway store, Geo. Tp
Lyons, William	33	Illinois	Dairyman	Lake Valley Township.
Lievre, Austin	33	Missouri	Butcher	Gold Hill.
Livingston, David McG	48	N. Hampshire	Board'g h k'per	Grizzly Flat.
Luce, George Washington	50	Kentucky	Teamster	Indian Diggings.
Leonard, John G	36	Pennsylvania	Miner	Mud Springs Township.
Lee, Henry Clay	33	Indiana	Farmer	El Dorado.
Lerch, Reuben	39	Pennsylvania	Miner	Georgetown Township.
Levmine, Leon	45	France	Stone cutter	" "
Lytle, Francis Marion	22	Maine	Farmer	Diamond Sp'gs "

M

NAMES.	Age	Place of Nativity.	Occupation.	Local Residence.
Meikle, James	28	Scotland	Miner	Grizzly Flat.
McHatton, John	40	Ireland	Merchant	Diamond Springs.
McFaden, John	51	Pennsylvania	Miner	White Oak Township.
McPherson, Thos. Henry	22	Virginia	Farmer	" " "
McCanahan, James Wm.	22	Kentucky	Butcher	" " "
McMurry, Jas. Douglass	39	Tennessee	Deputy Sheriff	Placerville "
Munson, John Phenias	40	New York	School Teacher	White Oak "
Martin, Nelson	29	Missouri	Miner	" " "
McClure, Thos. Greenfield	38	Ohio	"	" " "
Mabee, Harvey Wills	39	Michigan	Farmer	" " "
McMannis, Thomas	39	New York	Merchant	Kelsey "
Mayer, George	50	Bavaria	Miner	Placerville "
Miller, Jos. Jno. Andrew	36	Pennsylvania	Ranchman	" "
Maynard, William Harris	40	England	Farmer	Diamond Springs "
Meacham, Benjamin	40	Ohio	Merchant	Placerville "
McCusker, Michael	44	Ireland	Road Overseer	" "
Mierson, Augustus	32	Prussia	Merchant	" "
Misteli, John Joseph	45	Switzerland	Miner	White Oak "
McKeehan, Alex. Frank'n	36	Tennessee	"	Mud Springs "
Murphy, Daniel	35	Ireland	"	" " "
Myer, Peter George	40	Denmark	Musician	Coloma "
Morrill, Smith	51	N. Hampshire	Farmer	Diamond Springs "
Montgomery, Callin	35	Ohio	Miner	Coloma "
Moseley, Albert Sanders	30	Massachusetts	Farmer	" "
Myers, Peter	30	Vermont	Printer	Placerville "
McCuen, Charles	40	Scotland	Miner	" "
Maxey, Jesse Blackman	48	Virginia	Farmer	Coloma.
Maginess, Samuel	50	Pennsylvania	Miner	Placerville Township.
McNaughton, Charles D.	35	New York	Teacher	Latrobe.
McFadden, John	36	Ireland	Ditch Agent	Coloma Township.
McThee, Duncan	36	Great Britain	" "	" "
McKeon, William	50	Pennsylvania	Engineer	Placerville "
Merrill, Oliver	40	Massachusetts		Coloma "
McBride, Barney	36	Great Britain	Saloon-keeper	" "
McFarlin, Solon Lycurgus	33	Ohio	Photographer	Placerville "
McBride, Robert Bennett	35	New York	Merchant	" "
McFarnahan, John Cowan	38	Ohio	Farmer	Coloma "
McConnaha, Benj. Frauk.	29	Indiana	Hostler	Placerville "
Miller, Thomas	40	Wirtemburg	Farmer	" "
McCormick, William	33	Ireland	Saloon-keeper	" "
McKay, Robert Conaughy	33	Ireland	Farmer	Coloma "
Moore, Saul	35	Pennsylvania	Clerk	Placerville "
McClure, James Simond	33	Pennsylvania	Speculator	" "
Murphy, Sylvester	37	Ireland	Hotel-keeper	" "
Miller, Thomas	24	Indiana	Farmer	Mud Springs "
Miller, James	32	Indiana	Laborer	Placerville "
McGrau, John	41	Ireland	Assessor & Col.	Kelsey "
Mason, Henry George	35	England	Gardener	Placerville "
Mong, George Painter	52	Virginia	Miner	" "
McLean, Charles Clinton	34	New York	Butcher	Mountain "
McFarnahan, Samuel Bar.	40	Ohio	Miner	Placerville "
McCuen, James	75	Scotland	"	" "
McGowan, Robert	47	Ireland	"	" "
Mebren, Jacob	37	Prussia	"	" "
Metzler, Mathias Charles	43	Germany	Butcher	" "
Mathews, Sam'l Augustus	41	West Indies	Miner	" "
Mallat, John	43	Switzerland	Lime Manuf'r	Greenwood "
Milham, Benedict	33	Switzerland	" "	" "
Miles, William Jackson	34	Indiana	Farmer	Diamond Springs Tp.
Mull, George	43	North Carolina	Miner	Placerville "

NAME.	Age	Place of Nativity.	Occupation.	Local Residence.
McCumsey, William	36	Ohio	Farmer	Placerville Township
Melvin, Abraham Taylor	47	N. Hampshire	Gas manufact'r	" "
Manning, David	42	Tennessee	Carpenter	" "
Moore, R. Gust's Romeus	58	Ohio	Miner	" "
Manefee, Nimrod William	39	Virginia	Rancher	" "
Manefee, Arthur Livings'n	27	Missouri	Wood-chopper	" "
Morris, Oliver Vinton	33	Pennsylvania	Shoemaker	" "
Michling, Michael	43	Pennsylvania	Hostler	" "
Murgotten, Henry Charles	50	Maryland	Carpenter	" "
McAllister, Thos. Wm	35	Virginia	Lumberman	" "
McKenzie, Roderick Dhu	27	Missouri	"	" "
Myers, Michael Limerick	30	Ohio	"	" "
Macomber, Philander Wm	32	Massachusetts	Miner	" "
Meek, Basil Edward	34	Indiana	Teamster	" "
Macomber, James Edwin	33	Massachusetts	Miner	" "
McCall, John Warren	34	Pennsylvania	Farmer	" "
McNelby, Patrick	32	Ireland	Miner	Coloma "
McCurdy, Robert	57	Ireland	Farmer	Georgetown "
Miller, Joseph	49	Baden	Miner	Newtown.
Meyer, George	37	Hanover	Hotel Keeper	Placerville Township
Miller, John	28	Austria	Miner	Coloma "
Maxwell, Michael	60	Ireland	Farmer	Placerville "
Munn, Joseph	36	Ohio	Teamster	" "
Melton, Amon	46	Ohio	Miner	Grizzly Flat.
McLagan, Thomas	43	Scotland	Merchant	Greenwood Township
Maguire, John	32	Ireland	Currier	Placerville "
Marshall, James Franklin	31	Kentucky	Speculator	" "
Moon, James	52	England	Miner	Kelsey "
Moss, Francis	39	Kentucky	Blacksmith	Diamond Sp. "
Monet, Louis J. Baptiste	42	France	Merchant	" "
Miller, James Cratcher	56	Kentucky	Miner	Coloma "
Miller, Samuel Rolin	48	Kentucky	"	" "
Miller, Nichol S.	30	Indiana	"	" "
Mason, Benjamin Dorsey	32	Maryland	"	" "
Maltby, Isaac	46	Connecticut	Farmer	White Oak "
Mathews, John Posey	40	Virginia	Miner	Kelley Creek.
McNaughton, Stwiges	40	Ohio	"	Fair Play.
Miles, Reuben	38	Vermont	Farmer	Placerville Township
Mountjoy, Columbus W	53	Kentucky	Hotel Keeper	" "
Morey, Benjamin Franklin	38	New York	Clerk	" "
McDonald, Bryan	35	Virginia	Miner	" "
McNoss, James Randolph	31	Georgia	"	" "
Meinking, Frederick	34	Germany	"	Greenwood "
McMasters, James	42	Ireland	"	Gold Hill.
McCarty, Daniel	35	Canada	"	Shingle Springs.
McKusick, Harrison J	34	Maine	"	Georgetown Township
Maddox, Findley Leonard	45	Kentucky	Attor'y at Law	" "
Mack, George Franklin	22	Illinois	Student	Placerville "
Mathews, Henry	36	Maine	Mason	Diamond Sp. "
Mayfield, Wayne	32	Tennessee	Miner	Georgetown "
Manning, William	42	Connecticut	Merchant	" "
Madden, John Elisha	28	South Carolina	Miner	" "
Morgan, Bart	38	Indiana	Ditch Agent	" "
Martin, John Taylor	50	Ohio	Miner	" "
Maxfield, George	53	Kentucky	Farmer	" "
Murzo, William	42	Virginia	Miner	" "
Martin, Joseph	30	Missouri	Farmer	" "
McCullough, Isaac	41	Pennsylvania	Miner	" "
McConnaha, Jas. Batson	57	Virginia	Landlord	Lake Valley "
Merrill, Lewis	31	Maine	Driver	" " "
Marsh, Alfred	29	Ohio	Laborer	" " "
Milliser, Samuel	55	Illinois	Hotel-keeper	" " "
Mosely, Albert	56	Connecticut	Farmer	Coloma "

NAMES.	Age	Place of Nativity.	Occupation.	Local Residence.
Mansfield, Nathan Eugene	38	Connecticut	Ditch Owner	Coloma Township.
McCarty, Alfred	39	Missouri	Miner	" "
Moore, Lewis Hickman	30	Tennessee	Rancher	Kelsey "
Martin, David	66	Delaware	"	" "
McGee, Edward	36	Ohio	Miner	" "
McFarland, Arch. "R."	44	New York	Water Agent	Diamond Springs Tp
McLaughlin, Jas. Armst'g	38	Indiana	Blacksmith	" "
Morris, William	61	Kentucky	Farmer	" "
Messmore, Jonas	36	Ohio	Laborer	" "
McClelland, John Stewart	34	Indiana	Miner	" "
Muffley, William Napp	40	Pennsylvania	Express Agent	" "
McKean, West Harris	34	Missouri	Miner	Indian Diggings.
Miller, Alexander	31	New York	"	Perry's Creek.
Martin, Caleb	38	Kentucky	"	Fair Play.
May, James	53	Tennessee	"	French Ranch.
Merrow, Josiah	29	Maine	"	Coyoteville.
Martin, William	54	Pennsylvania	Store-keeper	Pilot Hill.
Myers, Louis Bloom	53	Pennsylvania	Farmer	Greenwood.
Martin, Andrew	37	Tennessee	Miner	Pilot Hill.
Morehead, Samuel Alex	34	Virginia	Teamster	" "
Manning, M. Manning	44	New York	Farmer	" "
Morehead, Jas. Anderson	30	New York	Miner	" "
Mud, George Bolivar	37	Maryland	"	" "
McComber, Wm. Blake	29	Massachusetts	"	Greenwood.
Miller, David	58	Pennsylvania	Farmer	Missouri Flat.
Miller, James Harrison	43	Tennessee	"	Latrobe.
McFee, Augustus Wm	33	Maine	Miner	El Dorado.
Marks, Daniel William	35	New York	Saloon Keeper	Kingsville.
Morris, Thomas "T"	66	Delaware	Laborer	Shingle Springs.
McCormick, James	34	Pennsylvania	Justice of Peace	El Dorado.
McClure, Jona. Stevens	45	N. Hampshire	Merchant	Shingle Springs.
McDowell, John Henry	37	Pennsylvania	Miner	Duncan's Store.
Marx, Louis	28	Missouri	Blacksmith	Shingle Springs.
Moseley, Beverly Allen	36	Missouri	Miner	Duncan's Store.
Morrelle, Franklin T	36	New York	School teacher.	El Dorado.
McCord, Francis Marion	32	Illinois	Miner	" "
Madden, Richard Ashmore	40	S. Carolina	"	Smith's Flat.
Meyer, Joseph	36	Switzerland	"	Grizzly Flat.
Maddux, James Henry	33	Illinois	Clergyman	Placerville Township.
Marks, Leander Douglass	45	New York	Butcher	" "
Melton, John	34	Indiana	"	Grizzly Flat.
Myers, Henry	36	Germany		
Mortensen, Ernest Fred. M	36	Germany	Farmer	Coloma Township.
Melchior, A. Michaels	37	Pennsylvania	Miner	Kelsey "
McClure, William	38	Ohio	Laborer	Diamond Sp'gs "
McKinney, J. Washington	33	Missouri	Miner	Georgetown "
McKeney, John	72	New York	Gentleman	" "
Marrs, Newton Franklin	45	Tennesseee	Miner	" "
McKay, John	58	Ireland	Farmer	Placerville "
Merrill, Charles Edward	33	Massachusetts	Ditch Agent	Coloma "
McQuiston, Thomas	40	Great Britain	Carpenter	Mud Springs "
Milege, Peter	27	Turkey	Miner	Placerville "
McIntosh, George	47	Maine	"	Georgetown "
Miller, John	46	Hanover	"	" "
Maxfield, Robert Banks	28	Kentucky	Farmer	" "
Maxfield, Gurshom	22	Missouri	Teamster	" "
Morrow, James	37	Great Britain	Miner	" "
Myers, Andreas	50	Prussia	Brewer	" "
Moosher, Jacob	40	Switzerland	Millwright	" "
McMahom, Patrick	43	Ireland	Miner	" "
Murphy, Richard	45	Ireland	"	" "
Morgan, Patrick	40	Ireland	"	" "
Moore, George Hedgpeth	56	Georgia	"	

NAME.	Age	Place of Nativity.	Occupation.	Local Residence.
Murphy, Patrick	33	Ireland	Miner	Georgetown Township.
Middleton, James	32	Illinois	"	" "
McCrub, Alexander	35	Ireland	"	Greenwood "
McNeight, William	44	Ireland	"	" "
Mallon, Phillip	33	Ireland	"	Salmon Falls "
Marshall, John	34	Scotland	"	Greenwood "
Maiyer, William	35	Bavaria	Farmer	Coloma "
Martin, "B. M."	35	Ireland	"	" "
Mitchell, Thomas	57	Great Britain	Miner	" "
Muller, George	40	Wirtemburg	Farmer	" "
Mitchell, Paul	38	England	Express Agent	" "
McBeath, James	35	Scotland	Saloon-keeper	" "
Meder, John	39	Luxemburg	Miner	White Oak "
Murray, Thomas	35	Ireland	Farmer	" " "
Myer, Rudolph	47	Germany	Miner	" " "
Monday, Phillip	46	Germany	"	" " "
Menke, Gerhard	39	Germany	Farmer	Salmon Falls "
Maylo, Francisco	36	Portugal	"	" " "
Martens, Christian	36	Hanover	Blacksmith	" " "
Murphy, Patrick Francis	37	Ireland	Farmer	" " "
Meyer, Franz	44	Prussia	Hotel keeper	Mud Springs "
McDermit, Bartholomew	62	Ireland	Gardener	" " "
McDaniel, George	60	Ireland	Farmer	" " "
McDaniel, John	35	Ireland	"	" " "
Maguire, John	31	Ireland	Railroad Agent	" " "
McAfee, Alex. Hanson	37	Pennsylvania	Laborer	Grizzly Flat.
Morey, Edward Rutledge	34	Ohio	Miner	" "
McKecknie, Andrew	41	Maine	"	" "
Mosar, John Ror	40	Germany	"	Cosumnes Township.
McCarril, Michael	37	Ireland	Farmer	" "
Murray, Hugh	39	Ireland	Miner	" "
Merkindollar, Geo. Peter	40	France	Teamster	" "
Mansfield, George	46	Nassau	Miner	" "
Myers, George	56	Germany	Shoemaker	" "
Mandl, Joseph	50	Wirtemburg	"	" "
McBeath, Robert	41	Scotland	Miner	White Oak "
Mafly, John	35	Great Britain	"	Mud Springs "
McManus, Patrick	37	Ireland	Farmer	" " "
McCausland, David	57	Ireland	Merchant	" " "
Metcalf, Patrick	46	Ireland	Farmer	" " "
Metcalf, John	29	Ireland	Miner	" " "
Maguire, Charles Smith	35	Massachusetts	"	" " "
Meagher, John	35	Great Britain	"	" " "
McCord, Joseph Warren	26	Arkansas	"	Diamond Springs T'p.
Mangold, Martin	46	Baden	Mason	" "
McDowell, Jos. Calhoun	30	Indiana	Stage driver	Placerville "
Monroe, George	30	Maine	Blacksmith	Lake Valley "
Marquart, Michael	33	Wirtemburg	Store-keeper	Coloma "
McCoy, James	55	Pennsylvania	Merchant	Georgetown "
Mitchell, John "T."	60	France	Miner	Diamond "
McClellan, John	40	Scotland	Laborer	Lake Valley "
Mum, Milton	29	New York	Teamster	Diamond Springs "
Means, Robert	31	Ireland	Miner	Coloma "
Meir, Henreich	30	Denmark	"	Kelsey "
Morys, Joseph	32	Austria	"	White Oak "
Margenia, Augustine	45	Switzerland	"	Placerville "
McConnell, Orlando H	40	Ohio	"	" "
Marces, Alva Woods	34	Maine	"	" "
Murphy, James	46	Ireland	"	Coloma "
Murray, Patrick	35	Ireland	Farmer	Salmon Falls "
Murray, Benj. Franklin	43	Missouri	Carpenter	Placerville "
Mosher, John	33	New York	Miner	Mud Springs "
McLerey, Peter	33	England	Farmer	White Oak "

NAME.	Age	Place of Nativity.	Occupation.	Local Residence.
Miller, George	38	Germany	Butcher	Shingle Sp'gs Towns'p
Miller, John	41	Germany	Farmer	Placerville "
McCurdy, Edward	22	Great Britain	"	Georgetown "
Magill, John Milton	32	Indiana	Miner	Placerville "
McCall, Thomas	49	Great Britain	"	Georgetown "
Musser, Pleasant Jefferson	48	Virginia	"	Lake Valley "
McGrail, Thomas	28	Ireland	"	Cosumnes "
Mallard, Benjamin	59	England	"	Coloma "
McCleran, John Harris	42	Kentucky	"	Georgetown "
Morgan, William	26	Missouri	Saloon keeper	" "
McTamahan, Isaac Con'ly	38	Ohio	Miner	Coloma "
Mock, Noah Phillip	20	North Carolina	"	Georgetown "
Moore, John Dunham	43	Maine	"	" "
Marshall, Frank	55	N. Hampshire	"	" "
Marshall, William Burns	37	Indiana	"	" "
McKoy, Hubbard Wilson	48	Vermont	Lumberman	" "
McKoy, Robert	56	Vermont	Farmer	" "
McKoy, Gaudencio Hub'd	25	Vermont	Lumberman	" "
Manning, Wm. Rensalair	43	Connecticut	Printer	" "
Maglue, Edward	45	Massachusetts	Miner	" "
Martin, William Frederick	24	Indiana	"	" "
McCoy, Felix	37	New York	Saloon keeper	Diamond Sp'gs "
Morse, Sylvester Hutch'n	39	Maine	Carpenter	Sly Park.
Mayon, William Henry	39	Indiana	Ditch Agent	Diamond Sp'gs "
Marshall, James Wilson	55	New Jersey	Farmer	Coloma "
More, Joseph	55	Pennsylvania	"	" "
McClane, Wiley Loftus	40	Georgia	Miner	" "
Morse, Augustus Hollowa	51	Maine		" "
McLean, William Nelson	37	Illinois	Laborer	Shingle Springs.
Maddux, James Thomas	36	Kentucky	"	El Dorado.
Markly, David	33	Illinois	Miner	"
Mathews, Francis Marion	36	Missouri	"	Nashville.
Miller, Nicholas William	25	Indiana	"	El Dorado.
Miller, David Peter	29	Indiana	"	"
McClure, Samuel Miller	40	South Carolina	Laborer	"
Morrison, Richard Tidings	37	Virginia	Miner	"
Miller, John Sanford	37	Dist. Columbia	Merchant	Latrobe.
Moessner, Christian Fred	40	Germany	Brewer	Coloma.
McCoy, Wilburn	37	Tennessee	Miner	Fair Play.
Murray, Richard	28	Pennsylvania	Stonecutter	Indian Diggings.
Mills, Hiram	33	New York	Miner	Fair Play.
McCloud, William	54	Ohio	Laborer	Diamond Sp's Town.
Miller, James Peter	31	Indiana	Miner	White Oak "
Morris, Benj. Franklin	35	Ohio	Farmer	Placerville "
McCormick, William	53	Pennsylvania	"	Lake Valley "
Murphy, John	22	Ohio	Miner	White Oak "
Markle, John Alexander	40	Pennsylvania	"	Kelsey "
Mills, John	60	New York	"	" "
McPherson, Henry Thos	27	Wisconsin	Farmer	Pilot Hill.
Martin, John Strange	35	Indiana	Miner	" "
Miller, George	38	Ohio		Placerville Township.
Methrin, David	36	Scotland	Painter	" "
McKean, William Sargent	22	Ohio	Engineer	" "
Macomber, David Wheeler			Farmer	" "
McFall, William	45	Pennsylvania	Blacksmith	" "
Miller, George Franklin	27	Indiana	Miner	" "
McAfee, Alexander Hanna	36	Pennsylvania	"	Mountain "
McLean, John Marion	29	Missouri	"	" "
McGuire, William	22	New York	Laborer	" "
McLean, James	42	Kentucky	Miner	" "
Martin, Michael	28	Michigan	"	" "
Marshall, James	32	Missouri	"	" "
Marshall, Robert	38	Virginia	"	Mud Springs "

NAME.	Age	Place of Nativity.	Occupation.	Local Residence.
Moore, Jonathan Wesley..	27	Tennessee	Miner	Kelsey Township.
May, Jacob	35	Bavaria	"	Cosumnes "
Mayer, Michael	26	Wirtemburg	Blacksmith	Placerville "
McMannus, Thomas "F"	38	Ireland	Miner	Kelsey "
McKinstry, Lee	47	Connecticut	"	Georgetown "
Morlan, Stephen Richard..	43	Ohio	"	Diamond Spr'gs "
Martin, Hamilton	30	Canada	Blacksmith	Placerville "
Meyer, Joseph	23	Germany	Farmer	Diamond Spr'gs "
Moss, James	34	England	"	" "
Mayers, Samuel	39	Pennsylvania	Miner	Placerville "
Murdock, John Alexander	45	Ireland	Farmer	" "
Mulloy, Peter	36	England	Clerk	Shingle Springs "
Morgan, Mat	31	Missouri	Saloon-keeper	Georgetown "
Martin, James Franklin	32	Georgia	Miner	" "
Meddock, Oliver Perry	38	Ohio	"	" "
Marcum, Thomas	57	Virginia	"	" "
Martin, Alexander	37	Georgia	"	" "
Miller, John Stebins	47	New York	"	Sly Park.
Marshall, Alexander	33	Kentucky	"	Pleasant Valley.
Mead, William Harmon	32	New York	Carpenter	Sly Park.
Mosher, Ethan	28	Michigan	Laborer	Placerville Township
Manning, Judson	27	Massachusetts	Carpenter	" "
Macomber, Leonard Wm..	32	Massachusetts	Miner	" "
McClure, Thos. Greenfield	40	Ohio	"	" "
Morlan, Samuel Erwin	45	Ohio	"	Diamond Spr'gs "
Marquard, George	44	Germany	Store-keeper	Gold Hill.
Mason, William Price	39	Dis. Columbia	Miner	Kelsey Township.
McDougall, Robert H	33	Scotland	"	White Oak "
Moloney, James	33	Ireland	"	Georgetown "
McCormack, Francis	38	Ireland	Saloon-keeper	" "
McKeon, Alexander	30	New York	Livery-keeper	Placerville "
Martin, Edward	39	England	Butcher	Mud Springs "
Maynard, Richard	37	Great Britain	Miner	Placerville "
McQuillen, Brian	35	Ireland	"	" "
Maynard, Charles	43	England	"	" "
Menefee, Arthur Clay	27	Missouri	Laborer	" "
Myer, John	50	Baden	Farmer	Diamond Spr'gs "
Morey, Roswell Evander..	26	Maine	Engineer	Lake Valley "
McComber, Freeman	36	New York	Hotel-keeper	" "
Munson, Joseph	40	Pennsylvania	Butcher	Coloma "
Munson, Jonas Ranle	46	Pennsylvania	Cattle Drover	" "
Murdick, Leonard Gibs	34	Ohio	Teamster	" "
McGuire, John Calhoun..	45	Alabama	Saloon-keeper	Grizzly Flat.
Massey, Benj. Franklin	34	South Carolina	Carpenter	El Dorado.
McMurphy, Archibald	52	New York	Laborer	"
Marsh, James Thomas	59	New York	Miner	Latrobe.
Mellinger, Geo. Wash't'g	45	Ohio	"	King's Store.
McAdams, Henry	33	Illinois	"	El Dorado.
Miller, Daniel	57	Pennsylvania	Farmer	"
Moore, Joshua	54	Kentucky	Hotel-keeper	"
Miles, Walter	42	Indiana	Farmer	"
McGee, John	35	Kentucky	Miner	Shingle Springs.
Massa, Antonio	30	Italy	"	Newtown.
Murgotten, Alex. Phillip..	21	Indiana	Printer	Placerville.
Mathews, Chas. William..	52	Nova Scotia	Carpenter	Mud Springs.
Miller, William	40	Germany	Miner	Spanish Flat.
Moore, John Thomas	55	Ohio	Hotel-keeper	Placerville.
Maze, John	51	Ohio	"	" "
Mack, George Franklin	21	Illinois	Hostler	" "
McMurtry, L. Campbell	50	Kentucky	Landlord	" "
Mette, Charles Anthony..	28	Michigan	Blacksmith	" "
Moherter, Alexander	34	Ohio	Farmer	Georgetown "
McClain, Lewis Brown	54	Maryland	Carpenter	" "

NAME.	Age	Place of Nativity.	Occupation.	Local Residence.
Mette, Henry	33	Hanover	Farmer	Salmon Falls.
Minor, Henry	30	New York	Bar-keeper	Placerville.
Margineeti, Carlo	50	Switzerland	Miner	Georgetown.
Mullen, Martin	37	Great Britain	"	Kelsey.
Miller, Daniel Peter	21	Indiana	"	Mud Springs Township.
Miller, David Key	23	Indiana	"	" " "
Morrison, James	50	Atlantic Ocean	Carpenter	Placerville "
Morgan, James	35	Great Britain	Farmer	Greenwood "
Mulick, Nicholas	45	France	Miner	Placerville "
Magini, Giovani	35	Switzerland	"	Georgetown "

N

NAME.	Age	Place of Nativity.	Occupation.	Local Residence.
Nighart, Daniel "P."	26	Ohio	Miner	White Oak Township.
Newell, Hugh Bell	34	Kentucky	Farmer	Coloma "
Nachman, Adolphus	43	Russia	Merchant	Placerville "
Nuss, George	39	Bavaria	Hotel-keeper	" "
Newell, William Henry	33	Connecticut	Miner	Kelsey "
Nordhaussenn, Henry	39	Bavaria	Laborer	Placerville "
Nash, Isaac Henry	36	Ohio	Merchant	" "
Noble, Robert	45	England	Millman	Georgetown "
Naper, Joy Howland	45	Ohio	Miner	Placerville "
Norris, William Craig	43	Virginia	Wood chopper	" "
Nugent, Thomas Carr	43	Indiana	Water Agent	" "
Nichol, Kelsa Jimeson	35	Pennsylvania	Miner	Coloma "
Norris, Joseph Spencer	23	Missouri	Farmer	Uniontown "
Norris, William	35	Ohio	Miner	" "
Nelson, Hiram Franklin	33	Massachusetts	"	Rose Springs.
Neff, Jerome	30	Michigan	"	Placerville Township.
Nightingale, James	43	England	"	Latrobe.
Nagler, Charles	37	France	Merchant	Greenwood Township.
Nelson, William	53	Kentucky	Minor	Georgetown "
Nott, Samuel Alphonso	28	Ohio	Telegrapher	Lake Valley "
Norris, John Tiner	61	South Carolina	Farmer	Uniontown.
Norris, Robert	39	Ohio	"	Diamond Springs T'p.
Nance, Henry	40	Illinois	"	" " "
Nelson, Adam	32	Pennsylvania	Laborer	Coyoteville.
Norton, James	42	New York	Miner	Brownsville.
Newell, Robert	26	Iowa	"	Pilot Hill.
Newhall, H. Thompson	40	Massachusetts	"	Greenwood Valley.
Newell, Sem	22	Iowa	"	Pilot Hill.
Norville, Wm. Freeman	39	Kentucky	"	" "
Nahlle, Andrew Harvey	22	Arkansas	Teamster	Shingle Springs.
Norton, David Edson	36	New York	Butcher	El Dorado.
Nichols, Jeremiah	38	Pennsylvania	Farmer	"
Norman, Henry	37	Prussia	Laborer	Fair Play.
Nichols, Ransom Marshal	37	Georgia	Miner	Georgetown Township.
Nunes, Manuel	54	Portugal	Farmer	" "
Nattrass, Cuthburt	55	England	Miner	Greenwood "
Nelson, Peter	46	Denmark	"	" "
Newman, John	42	Prussia	"	Georgetown "
Nattrass, Joseph Burn	23	Wisconsin	Teamster	" "
Nicolaison, John	33	Denmark	Miner	Coloma "
Nelson, George	27	Ireland	Farmer	" "
Neibur, August	42	Prussia	Miner	Grizzly Flat.
Nift, Frederick	40	Prussia	"	White Oak Township.
Nicholls, William	24	England	"	Coloma "
Nicholls, Francis	30	England	"	" "
Nelson, Robert	39	Denmark	"	Diamond Springs T'p.
Nelson, Ole Christian	48	Denmark	"	" " "
Noyes, Loring Dudley	37	New York	"	Placerville "
Neale, Lewis Underwood	43	Virginia	"	" "
Noles, James Palmer	50	Maine	"	Georgetown "

NAMES.	Age	Place of Nativity.	Occupation.	Local Residence.
Norvell, Rufus Morgan	51	Tennessee	Miner	Georgetown Township.
Nye, Samuel Porter	41	Massachusetts	Farmer	"
Newell, William Pen	30	Illinois	Miner	Gold Hill.
Nixon, Robert	45	Pennsylvania	Teamster	Latrobe.
Nichol, Andrew Jackson	43	Pennsylvania	Miner	White Oak Township.
Norris, Newton Perry	49	Kentucky	"	Mountain "
Neff, Harry "H"	64	New York	"	Placerville "
Neff, Jerome	30	Michigan	Teamster	" "
Newhall, Augustus Brew	45	Pennsylvania	Miner	Salmon Falls "
Noyes, Eliphalet	50	Maine	"	" "
Nail, Mathias	62	Virginia	"	Grizzly Flat.
Newland, William	55	Kentucky	Farmer	Shingle Springs.
Norris, Andrew Jackson	38	Virginia	"	Placerville Township.

O

NAMES.	Age	Place of Nativity.	Occupation.	Local Residence.
Osgood, Nemie	46	N. Hampshire	Supt. Toll Road	Lake Valley Township.
Owens, Daniel	36	Ireland	Baker	Placerville "
Ollis, Henry	34	Germany	Blacksmith	" "
O'Malley, James	51	Ireland	Miner	Coloma "
O'Bannon, Charles	32	Virginia	"	Placerville "
O'Donnell, James	36	Ireland	"	Coloma "
Orr, Thomas	65	Scotland	Farmer	Salmon Falls "
Overmyer, Benj. Franklin	29	Indiana	Laborer	Placerville "
Overmyer, Edward	23	Wisconsin	Farmer	" "
Ober, Isaac	45	Pennsylvania	"	" "
Olmsted, Rufus Henry	31	New York	Miner	" "
Owen, Watson William	45	New York	Farmer	" "
Olson, Eric	46	Sweden	Miner	" "
Oakley, Aaron Doty	25	New York	Shoemaker	" "
O'Rourke, Barney	48	Ireland	Laborer	" "
O'Brien, James Garlin	34	Kentucky	Farmer	Cold Springs.
Owens, Nelson	54	New York	Blacksmith	Georgetown.
Owen, David	35	New York	Miner	Diamond Springs.
Oxley, Jas. Montgomery	37	Kentucky	"	South Fork.
Owens, Thomas	38	New York	"	Greenwood Township.
Olds, Horace Pringle	26	New York	Merchant	El Dorado.
O'Hale, Henry	28	Ohio	Millwright	" "
Ostlin, Charles William	37	Finland	Miner	Kelsey Township.
Orr, Thomas	36	Scotland	Stage Driver	Georgetown "
Obrock, Frederick	47	Germany	Miner	Greenwood "
O'Leary, John	46	Great Britain	"	Grizzly Flat.
Ormston, James	40	England	"	Diamond Springs T'p
Organ, Thomas John	43	England	Lawyer	Mud Springs "
Oldfield, Thomas James	30	Illinois	Miner	Placerville "
Oldfield, John Francis	22	Wisconsin	"	" "
Oswald, Joseph	43	Germany	"	Diamond Sp'gs "
Orr, James Jackson	38	Scotland	Stage Agent	Salmon Falls "
O'Dell, Benj. Franklin	34	Ohio	Miner	Placerville "
Osbourne, Rufus Wales	32	Massachusetts	Shoemaker	Georgetown.
Othick, William David	47	Connecticut	Farmer	Coloma.
Ormsbee, Henry	41	Ohio	Mechanic	Indian Diggings.
Owen, Charles	24	Kentucky	Laborer	White Oak Township.
Olomore, Alexander	44	New York	"	Dicks' Ranch.
O'Bryan, William Perry	40	Kentucky	Miner	Sly Park.
Overmyer, Quincy Albert	21	Illinois	Teamster	White Oak Township.
Odell, Edward Loring	45	Canada	Laborer	Diamond Sp'gs "
O'Conner, George	42	Ireland	Miner	Mud Springs "
Olmsted, Chas. Hatfield	43	Maine	"	Salmon Falls "
O'Conor, John Hall	38	New York	Mason	" "
O'Connor, Michael	52	New York	Miner	Greenwood "
Otto, Daniel	59	Pennsylvania	"	Salmon Falls "
O'Hale, Edward	28	Ohio	Carpenter	Mud Springs "

NAME.	Age	Place of Nativity.	Occupation.	Local Residence.
O'Keefe, Michael	31	Ireland	Miner	Placerville Township.
Oberreich, Charles	37	Prussia	Merchant	Diamond Sp'gs "

P

NAME.	Age	Place of Nativity.	Occupation.	Local Residence.
Page, John	48	SouthCarolina	Shoemaker	White Oak Township.
Patterson, Robert	31	Pennsylvania	Farmer	" " "
Patterson, John	56	Pennsylvania	Miner	" " "
Patten, Hiram	28	Maine	"	Smith's Flat.
Porter, James Turley	41	Illinois	Road Overseer	Mud Springs "
Pinkham, John Franklin	41	New York	Farmer	Placerville "
Potochi, Charles	42	Switzerland	Miner	" "
Prescott, John	33	Massachusetts	Engineer	" "
Paulsmeier, Henry	37	Prussia	Miner	Grizzly Flat.
Pierce, Henry Baldwin	39	Vermont	Road Overseer	Coloma "
Phipps, William	28	Ohio	School Teacher	" "
Phillip, Louis	43	Russia	Tailor	Placerville "
Penwell, Sam. Alexander	34	Ohio	Teacher	Coloma "
Peirce, Charles Caleb	40	Ohio	Clergyman	Placerville "
Pettit, Charles Benjamin	36	Kentucky	Merchant	" "
Perry, Thomas	48	Wales	Miner	Coloma "
Pearson, Charles	42	Ohio	Tinner	Placerville "
Pratt, Irving Washington	31	New York	Teacher	" "
Patton, John Rufus	49	Pennsylvania	Miner	" "
Patton, James	37	Ireland	Blacksmith	" "
Powers, Henry Foster	29	N. Hampshire	Miner	" "
Pease, Victor Cicero	25	Ohio	School Teacher	Lake Valley "
Porter, William Comstock	39	New York	Farmer	Placerville "
Perkins, Franklin	38	New York	Carpenter	" "
Post, Benjamin Franklin	48	N. Hampshire	"	" "
Page, Horace Francis	32	New York	Livery Stable	" "
Peabody, Andrew Jackson	32	New York	Coach Trimmer	" "
Parker, Elias Levi	36	Massachusetts	Miner	" "
Pew, Benjamin Franklin	56	New York	Farmer	" "
Pittsford, William Henry	45	Kentucky	Rancher	" "
Pelton, Samuel Bradford	64	Massachusetts	Board'g h.keep.	White Oak "
Pearis, Robert Alexander	43	Virginia	Physician	Placerville "
Parkhurst, Oscar	30	New York	Merchant	" "
Pelton, Samuel Conger	28	Canada	Miner	White Oak "
Peter, Jacob	31	Ohio	"	Placerville "
Penders, James Daniel	30	New York	"	White Oak "
Patterson, William Lytle	32	Pennsylvania	"	Cold Springs.
Parker, William Henry	40	Maine	Blacksmith	Placerville "
Peck, William Bradley	26	Michigan	Lumberman	" "
Penter, Joseph	47	Tennessee	Farmer	" "
Pray, Ozro Dunham	42	Ohio	Miner	Diamond Spr'gs "
Prepmeyer, Jos. Francis	49	Germany	"	Coloma "
Pedrony, Peter	22	Switzerland	"	Placerville "
Patrick, George	45	England	"	Coloma "
Pierce, Simeon Otis	42	Maine	"	Shingle Springs.
Probert, William	46	England	"	Cosumnes Township.
Purslow, James Fox	34	England	"	Coloma "
Phipps, William	54	Kentucky	Farmer	Georgetown "
Porter, Marion Francis	32	Indiana	Miner	" "
Prince, Daniel	35	Massachusetts	"	" "
Perkins, William	44	Maryland	"	" "
Pratt, Merritt	42	New York	"	" "
Porter, Hiram More	46	Kentucky	"	" "
Pomeroy, James Allen	49	Kentucky	Farmer	" "
Parker, Allen George	27	Indiana	Driver	Strawberry.
Pierce, Charles Boyden	36	Massachusetts	Laborer	Lake Valley "
Phillips, Alden Church	29	Pennsylvania	Landlord	" "
Phillips, J. Wells Davis	38	Pennsylvania	"	" "

NAME.	Age	Place of Nativity.	Occupation.	Local Residence.
Powell, Elija	37	Illinois	Laborer	Lake Valley Township
Prince, Adam	45	Virginia	Miner	Salmon Falls "
Poor, John	38	N. Hampshire	"	Kelsey " "
Plummer, David	61	Vermont	"	" " "
Parks, Andrew	43	Ohio	"	" " "
Potter, Clark	49	New York	"	" " "
Phillips, Geo. Washington	41	Kentucky	Carpenter	Diamond Springs "
Parks, Aaron Davis	44	New Jersey	Carpenter	" " "
Perry, Elisha Hapgood	37	Massachusetts	Farmer	Brownsville.
Putnam, William Henry	30	N. Hampshire	"	Cedar Creek.
Putnam, James Anderson	45	N. Hampshire	"	" "
Pratt, Henry	40	Missouri	Miner	Spanish Creek.
Purinton, Henry Osgood	27	Maine	Store-keeper	Fair Play.
Parker, Alonzo Levi	33	Ohio	Miner	Pilot Hill.
Price, Joseph	31	New York	"	" "
Pendexter, John Langdon	34	N. Hampshire	"	" "
Platt, Elisha Wickes	55	New York	Farmer	" "
Page, Azor Newton	26	Maine	"	Greenwood
Pollard, Benj. Franklin	41	Maine	"	Greenwood
Penter, John Redman	25	Arkansas	Laborer	Latrobe.
Patten, Francis William	38	Massachusetts	Carpenter	Shingle Springs.
Plyler, Gabriel	38	South Carolina	Miner	Logtown.
Parmeter, Joel	28	Michigan	Teamster	Shingle Springs.
Perry, Warren Thatcher	34	Pennsylvania	"	Placerville.
Peckhart, Peter	43	Prussia	Miner	Clarksville.
Paiss, Henry	42	Germany	"	Diamond Springs.
Prongree, Joseph	47	Switzerland	Farmer	Cosumnes Township.
Pavey, Charles	60	England	"	Mud Springs "
Potts, Thomas	46	England	Miner	Placerville.
Palmer, John	35	Ohio	"	White Oak.
Parker, Charles Orin	37	New York	Farmer	Georgetown Township.
Perkins, Daniel Russel	44	Connecticut	Farmer	" "
Polhamus, Cornelius B	43	New York	Carpenter	" "
Parsons, George Wilson	45	England	Miner	" "
Porter, Loyd	29	Georgia	"	" "
Paulding, William	39	Canada	Tailor	" "
Peterson, Marcus	43	Denmark	Miner	Greenwood "
Prezehl, August	36	Hanover	"	" "
Peterson, Anton	36	Denmark	"	Coloma "
Peterson, And. Johnson	34	Denmark	"	" "
Pelton, Aylmer	35	Canada	"	White Oak.
Patterson, William	50	England	"	Salmon Falls.
Perrazzo, John Baptiste	61	Sardinia	Farmer	" "
Prescott, John	36	N. Hampshire	Engineer	" "
Plumb, Wallace Boardm'n	28	New York	Farmer	White Oak Township.
Pollock, Joseph	49	Ireland	Miner	Mud Springs "
Probasco, George Wash	40	Indiana	"	" "
Putnam, Albert	38	Massachusetts	Stage Driver	Placerville
Plucker, Bernard	32	Prussia	Lumberman	Grizzly Flat.
Palmer, Orange Spencer	37	New York	Carpenter	" "
Patterson, John	37	Scotland	Miner	Cosumnes Township.
Price, Richard	28	England	Farmer	Coloma "
Pavey, Geo. Washington	26	Michigan	"	Mud Springs Township.
Pavey, William Henry	38	England	Hotel-keeper	" "
Pope, John Christian	40	Hanover	Miner	Diamond Springs "
Pruetzel, Christian	44	Germany	"	" " "
Pruetzel, Louis	38	Germany	"	" " "
Parrish, Charles Halsey	30	New York	Blacksmith	Placerville "
Pett, Edwin	33	England	Miner	Mud Springs "
Penter, Geo. Washington	23	Arkansas	"	" "
Peters, Robert James	47	England	"	White Oak "
Plitcher, Wm. Frederick	31	Prussia	"	Mud Springs "
Potter, Paraclete	29	New York	"	Placerville

NAMES.	Age	Place of Nativity.	Occupation.	Local Residence.
Pietero, Pederolli	37	Switzerland	Miner	Coloma Township.
Peterson, Peter Michael	50	Denmark	"	" "
Painter, Jackson Ludlow	30	Ohio	"	Georgetown "
Painter, Adam Walter	36	Indiana	"	" "
Pease, Edwin	27	Illinois	Lumberman	" "
Purdy, Henry Bennett	37	New York	Miner	" "
Poorman, Hugh White	56	Pennsylvania	Farmer	Diamond Sp. "
Plumado, Francis Hilair	37	Canada	Ditch Agent	Placerville "
Poague, William Franklin	44	Virginia	Tailor	Coloma "
Poteet, Thomas Job	40	Indiana	Farmer	" "
Parker, Sewel Wilson	38	New York	Blacksmith	Shingle Springs.
Potter, Isaac Howland	52	Rhode Island	Gen'l Business	El Dorado.
Philips, Levi	33	New York	Laborer	Latrobe.
Porter, Nathaniel	35	Missouri	Farmer	"
Penter, William Carvasso	24	Arkansas	Laborer	"
Patterson, John	35	Ohio	Teamster	Shingle Springs.
Price, William Henry	43	New York	Blacksmith	" "
Penter, William Munday	49	Tennessee	Farmer	Latrobe.
Peters, Jacob	47	Pennsylvania	Teamster	Nashville.
Pollard, William Walker	38	Virginia	Miner	"
Perry, William Edward	46	Virginia	Saloon-keeper	El Dorado.
Phillipps, John	38	Pennsylvania	Miner	Fair Play.
Phibbs, Henry Clay	34	Ohio	"	Cosumnes Township.
Phibbs, John Quincy	34	Ohio	"	" " "
Pollock, William Henry	37	Tennessee	"	" " "
Platt, Charles Truesdell	26	Indiana	Farmer	Pilot Hill.
Parks, John West	32	New York	Miner	Greenwood Township.
Powers, Cyrus Perkins	38	New York	Teamster	Placerville "
Phelps, Theodore Edgar	33	Michigan	Miner	Mountain "
Palmer, Hiram	48	New York	"	" "
Perry, John Bolliver	33	New Jersey	"	" "
Phillips, Benjamin Russ'l	32	Virginia	"	" "
Pritchett, Zachariah	50	Ohio	Farmer	Smith's Flat.
Prodger, Chas. Matthew	21	England	Teleg'h ope'tor	Georgetown '
Parlow, Benjamin Glover	21	Massachusetts	Farmer	Placerville "
Pratt, Ephraim	46	Massachusetts	Miner	Georgetown "
Palmer, Anson	42	New York	Teamster	" "
Parberry, William Milton	44	Virginia	Miner	Diamond Sp. "
Payne, Henry	72	Virginia	Farmer	" "
Parberry, John Lewis	42	Virginia	Miner	" "
Pelton, Stephen	30	Canada	"	White Oak "
Payne, Peter Erlls	67	New York	Farmer	Placerville "
Phipps, James	40	England	Saddler	" "
Phelps, Wm. W. Brewster	21	Illinois	Laborer	Lake Valley "
Perkins, William	45	Maryland	Miner	Pilot Hill.
Palmer, Niles Ossian	38	Ohio	"	" "
Post, Wheeler	50	Tennessee	Laborer	Placerville Township.
Payton, John	27	Virginia	Miner	Grizzly Flat.
Pike, Jabez Tucker	54	Massachusetts	"	" "
Proctor, Francis Marion	36	Missouri	Farmer	Cosumnes Township.
Pargen, John C	34	Illinois	Miner	" "
Petree, Robert Elliott	38	Tennessee	Laborer	Latrobe.
Porter, William Thomas	34	Missouri	"	
Perrin, Solomon Clark	38	Kentucky	Landlord	Placerville Township.
Parker, Francis Addison	25	New York	Cook	" "
Parker, Courtland	38	Ohio	Blacksmith	" "
Penter, Reuben	22	Arkansas	Miner	" "
Pratt, Frank. Dennison	32	Maine	"	Georgetown "
Pesseles, Bernhard	29	Austria	Merchant	" "
Peter, Giovani	32	Switzerland	Miner	" "
Phelps, Charles	35	Vermont	"	Placerville.
Peters, Herman	52	Prussia	"	Greenwood Township.
Price, George	40	Missouri	"	Kelsey "

NAME.	Age	Place of Nativity.	Occupation.	Local Residence.
Pickett, Lewis	37	Missouri	Miner	White Oak Township.
Petar, Carlo	34	Switzerland	"	Georgetown "
Petty, John Stuart	28	Kentucky	"	Placerville "

Q

NAME.	Age	Place of Nativity.	Occupation.	Local Residence.
Quinn, John Devlin	39	Ireland	Freight Agent.	Shingle Springs.
Quesada, Luise	40	Mexico	Miner	Placerville.
Quanchi, Giulio	22	Switzerland	"	Coloma Township
Quanchi, Jacob	35	Switzerland	"	" "
Quirk, James	29	Great Britain	"	" "
Quary, Douglass	32	Pennsylvania	"	Placerville "

R

NAME.	Age	Place of Nativity.	Occupation.	Local Residence.
Rolleri, Joseph	48	Italy	Saloon-keeper	Placerville Township.
Richmond, John William	58	Virginia	Farmer	White Oak "
Richardson, Jackson Eben	42	South Carolina	Carpenter	" "
Rust, William Wallace	39	Massachusetts	Farmer	" "
Ramsey, Alexander	30	New York	"	" "
Raphael, Henry	24	Ohio	Merchant	Placerville "
Redington, Jacob Smith	33	New York	Tinner	" "
Roy, John	49	Scotland	Cabinetmaker	" "
Riebsam, William Erwin	36	Pennsylvania	Merchant	Latrobe.
Rasmussen, Andrew	42	Sweden	Farmer	Coloma Township.
Reed, John Irwin	34	Kentucky	Miner	" "
Roup, Alex. Willshire	44	Ohio	Farmer	" "
Reen, John	45	Great Britain	Miner	Mud Springs "
Reid, Alex. Hamilton	47	Maryland	Livery	Placerville "
Richardson, Geo. Washt'n	35	New York	Blacksmith	" "
Reeder, Louis	36	Germany	Farmer	" "
Ryan, Thomas	46	Ireland	Laborer	" "
Richardson, Luke Brown	38	Vermont	Merchant	" "
Robertson, Horatio Perry	30	Tennessee	Wood-chopper	" "
Rankin, Robert	46	Kentucky	Physician	" "
Reeg, Leonard	35	Germany	Bridge-keeper	Kelsey "
Raymond, Aug. Cezar	36	Ohio	Saddler	Placerville "
Reis, Henry	36	Prussia	Miner	" "
Roff, Henry L	21	Missouri	Express Clerk	" "
Rosier, Levi	42	New York	Miner	" "
Rupley, Theodore	25	Ohio	Farmer	" "
Regan, Cornelius	52	Tennessee	Miner	" "
Rockwell, Peter King	65	Vermont	Rancher	" "
Robinson, Saml. Quimley	37	Ohio	Miner	" "
Rothermand, Frd. Warner	36	Germany	Farmer	Salmon Falls "
Riemer, Frederick	59	Germany	"	White Oak "
Rice, George	31	Pennsylvania	Laborer	Placerville "
Ranney, George Childs	39	Connecticut	Carpenter	" "
Reese, John	44	Wales	Miner	" "
Rock, John Jacob	31	Illinois	Steward	" "
Rolland, Victor Joseph	31	France	Farmer	Placerville "
Richardson, James	36	Indiana	"	Diamond Spr'gs "
Russell, James Pennoyer	39	New York	Water Agent	Coloma "
Robinson, David	46	Virginia	Carpenter	Mud Springs "
Raffetti, Domenico	30	Italy	Farmer	Diamond Sp'gs "
Richmond, John Alex	21	Louisiana	Teamster	Clarksville.
Russell, Jas. Sanderson	36	Massachusetts	Miner	Pleasant Grove.
Robinson, Samuel Davis	38	Indiana	Farmer	Indian Diggings.
Robertson, John	39	Scotland	"	Clarksville.
Reynolds, James Madison	39	Kentucky	Miner	Placerville Township.
Rockwell, Wm. Russell	31	Pennsylvania	Water Agent	" "
Rau, George	40	Germany	Miner	Georgetown "
Robinson, Elija	44	Ohio	Teamster	Diamond Spr'gs "

NAMES.	Age	Place of Nativity.	Occupation.	Local Residence.
Rugg, Joel Lee	37	Pennsylvania	Miner	Greenwood Township.
Raymond, Harry Moore	36	Ireland	Hotel-keeper	" "
Roff, Sylvanus Pressey	36	Maine	Miner	Georgetown. "
Recker, Lemuel	29	Maine	"	" "
Russell, Henry Warren	36	Massachusetts	"	" "
Robinson, Edward	39	New York	"	" "
Ramsay, Lycurgus L	48	Missouri	Hunter	Strawberry Valley.
Ruland, Samuel	37	Missouri	Lawyer	Lake "
Ramsey, George William	37	Pennsylvania	Farmer	Uniontown.
Rohrer, Cyrus	43	Maryland	Hotel	Rolling Hills.
Rucker, Addison	40	Missouri	Miner	Kelsey Township.
Rich, Heath Peck	35	New York	"	" "
Rhodes, William Lustomb	43	Maryland	"	" "
Rives, John Johnson	55	Georgia	"	" "
Rader, John	42	Virginia	Blacksmith	Diamond Springs.
Reynolds, James Verley	51	New York	Saloon-keeper	" "
Robertson, Munson S	54	New York	Farmer	" "
Rogers, Alfred Henry	27	New York	Miner	" "
Rogers, Charles Edward	24	New York	"	" "
Rymal, Geo. Washington	33	Tennessee	Farmer	Cosumnes Township.
Roberdiere, Dominick	35	New York	Miner	" "
Richards, John Henry	30	Maine	Engineer	" "
Redding, Enoch	37	Illinois	Miner	" "
Remick, Merrill Nahum	34	Maine	Hotel-keeper	" "
Reppey, Jas. Washington	39	Missouri	Miner	" "
Rockey, Leonard	38	Illinois	"	" "
Read, Wilbur	55	Massachusetts	Farmer	Greenwood "
Rogers, Calvin Selden	38	Maine	Miner	" "
Robbins, Joseph Henry	42	Massachusetts	Carpenter	Shingle Springs.
Rapp, Charles William	34	New York	Miller	Latrobe.
Rose, John	55	Pennsylvania	Miner	Mud Springs Township.
Roussin, Chas. Theofield	32	Missouri	"	" " "
Root, James	40	Ohio	Hunter	" " "
Rolke, George Harmon	37	Maryland	Hotel-keeper	Kelsey "
Ramsey, Ebenezer Tate	38	Ohio	Miner	" "
Ressguie, Addesson	38	Vermont	Carpenter	Latrobe.
Rodefeld, John Henry	37	Germany	Shoemaker	Coloma Township.
Rowland, Thomas Benton	34	Vermont	Hotel-keeper	Strawberry Valley.
Rogers, James Madison	46	New York	Farmer	White Oak.
Rehder, Frederick	36	Denmark	Laborer	Sly Park.
Robinson, Peter	67	Vermont	Amalgamator	Kelsey Township.
Robins, Sylvester	47	Vermont	Cook	" "
Robson, John	51	Great Britain	Miner	Georgetown Township.
Riemenschreider, Henrich	38	Hesse Cassell	"	" "
Robson, Joseph	46	Great Britain	"	" "
Rook, Allin	42	England	"	" "
Rice, Andrew	38	Kentucky	"	" "
Ricci, Felici	41	Tuscany	Store-keeper	Greenwood "
Roussin, Cypian Leon	26	Missouri	Miner	Mud Springs "
Riley, John	40	Great Britain	"	White Oak "
Ryan, Price	41	Great Britain	Farmer	" " "
Roseleib, Laurence	61	Hanover	Gardener	Mud Springs "
Reed, Orange Dennis	43	Vermont	Teamster	" " "
Rush, William	35	New York	Forwarding Agt	" " "
Ryan, Michael	37	Ireland	Laborer	" " "
Richardson, Amos	68	Kentucky	"	Diamond Springs T'p.
Russell, Osborn	53	Maine	Miner	" " "
Riger, John	36	Germany	"	" " "
Raillard, Joseph	36	France	"	" " "
Russell, Daniel	39	Scotland	Farmer	Salmon Falls "
Reed, Elija	58	Pennsylvania	"	Mud Springs "
Russell, Thomas	38	Ireland	Trader	" " "
Rohrig, John Christian F.	43	Hanover	Farmer	Diamond Springs.

NAME.	Age	Place of Nativity.	Occupation.	Local Residence.
Rice, William	26	Iowa	Laborer	Placerville Township.
Rodahan, Bernard	56	Great Britain	Teacher	White Oak "
Rey, Ambrose	34	France	Teamster	Mud Springs "
Rutledge, Edward	39	Ireland	Miner	Gold Hill.
Reed, Caleb	36	Nova Scotia	"	Placerville Township.
Robinson, Hiram	33	Ireland	"	Latrobe.
Robinson, Edward	40	New York	"	Georgetown Township.
Ritchie, George	40	Ohio	Butcher	" "
Riley, Thomas Benton	26	Missouri	Lumberman	Diamond Springs T'p.
Richardson, Parson	49	New York	Farmer	" "
Reeves, John	57	South Carolina	"	Coloma.
Rodgers, James Henry	37	New York	Miner	El Dorado.
Richardson, Isaac B.	40	Tennessee	Dep. Assessor	" "
Robinson, Henry	30	Illinois	Teamster	" "
Raukin, John D.	46	Missouri	Miner	Nashville.
Reed, Warren Mills	40	Massachusetts	"	El Dorado.
Roland, John Howard	22	Ohio	Laborer	Cosumnes Township.
Richardson, Edw. Herbert	47	Ohio	Farmer	" "
Redd, Robert Harris	35	Virginia	Miner	Placerville "
Rice, Oscar	47	Pennsylvania	Farmer	White Oak "
Rentz, William Dodridge	25	Indiana	"	Lake Valley "
Ryburn, William Allen	38	Tennessee	Miner	Coloma "
Reynolds, Andrew Perry	32	Pennsylvania	"	Kelsey "
Ray, John Washington	53	Georgia	"	" "
Rebman, Joseph	34	Ohio	"	Greenwood "
Rose, James Holly	37	New York	"	Pilot Hill.
Robbins, Nathaniel	52	Massachusetts	"	Salmon Falls Township.
Russell, Charles	35	New York	Saddler	Placerville "
Reynolds, Franklin	39	New York	Miner	Mountain "
Richardson, Hiram David	35	Kentucky	"	" "
Richardson, Hezekiah M.	35	New York	Engineer	" "
Robinson, John	36	England	Miner	Mud Springs "
Reed, William	40	Pennsylvania	Cooper	Georgetown "
Rouner, James Lewis	38	Indiana	Miner	Gold Hill.
Richardson, Wm. Jourdin	38	Maine	"	Shingle Springs.
Rudduck, Thomas Daniel	30	England	"	Kelsey Township.
Russell, Hiram	55	New York	Shoemaker	Georgetown Township
Reyburn, John Dennis	44	Kentucky	Shingle-maker	Sly Park.
Rumsey, Edwin	36	New York	Teamster	" "
Reed, Samuel	46	Maine	Laborer	Placerville Township
Rice, Myron Munroe	28	Michigan	Miner	" "
Robards, Aaron Hatfield	33	Indiana	"	Diamond Springs T'p.
Rohan, Dennis	28	Ireland	"	Mud Springs "
Royen, John	35	Virginia	"	White Oak "
Randall, Henry Augustus	41	Rhode Island	"	" "
Robinson, George	43	England	"	Georgetown
Rose, Henry	47	Hanover	"	Placerville
Rice, John Mosby	40	Missouri	"	Georgetown
Roush, William	43	Pennsylvania	"	Greenwood
Roberts, Edward E.	33	Pennsylvania	"	Placerville
Rice, Nathaniel	47	Pennsylvania	"	"
Russell, Lawson Merrick	31	Vermont	"	Grizzly Flat.
Richardson, Wm. Jourdin	39	Maine	Farmer	Shingle Springs T'p.
Roise, Solomon	63	Kentucky	Laborer	El Dorado.
Rhoads, Richard Watts	61	Virginia	"	Nashville.
Rigsby, George Edward	28	Kentucky	Miner	El Dorado.
Rowley, Wm. Augustus	34	New York	"	" "
Righter, Michael	39	Pennsylvania	"	Shingle Springs.
Red, Charles	33	Wisconsin	"	Latrobe.
Rammer, Ludwe	36	Germany	"	Grizzly Flat.
Reinhold, Neils	34	Denmark	"	White Oak Township.
Robera, Jerome	40	Spain	"	Georgetown "
Roberts, Henry Hugh	36	Great Britain	"	Placerville "

NAME.	Age	Place of Nativity.	Occupation.	Local Residence.
Roanda, Guilio	28	Switzerland	Laborer	Diamond Springs T'p.
Russell, William Henry	42	Ireland	Miner	Georgetown "
Robinette, Eugine	40	France	Merchant	" "
Robb, Hamilton Dickey	51	Pennsylvania	Rancher	" "
Robb, John Alexander	21	Iowa	Dairyman	" "
Reboulet, Louis	37	France	Farmer	Cosumnes "
Romeli, Giovani	31	Switzerland	Bar-keeper	Georgetown "
Rupley, John Wesley	52	Pennsylvania	Farmer	Placerville "
Ralph, Thomas	43	Great Britain	Miner	" "

S

NAME.	Age	Place of Nativity.	Occupation.	Local Residence.
Squires, Ogden	35	New York	County Judge	Placerville Township.
Star, Benjamin	55	Connecticut	Carpenter	White Oak "
Smith, Edward Hall	35	Massachusetts	Merchant	" " "
Smith, Thomas Nelson	29	Massachusetts	Farmer	" " "
Strout, Enoch Noyes	43	Maine	Clerk	Placerville "
Schelkle, Maximlian	35	Wirtemburg	Carpenter	" "
Stewart, William Wallace	36	Pennsylvania	Merchant	" "
Swan, George Wheeler	44	N. Hampshire	Road Agent	" "
Sackrider, Christian	50	New York	Stage Driver	" "
Stephens, John Cowlin	38	England	Teamster	" "
Silberman, Phillip	36	Bavaria	Merchant	" "
Silberman, Chas. Arnold	38	Bavaria	"	" "
Showalter, Isaac	54	Pennsylvania	Farmer	Coloma "
Stevens, Varrannas P	28	Ohio	Miner	" "
Stearns, William	34	Massachusetts	Ditch Agent	" "
Stockdale, Robert F	30	Ohio	Stage driver	" "
Spencer, Richard T	49	Great Britain	Miner	Kelly Creek.
Schomp, Justus	30	Ohio	Teamster	Placerville.
Staffani, Henreci	30	Switzerland	Milkman	"
Seig, Frederick	50	Germany	Saloon-keeper	"
Standeford, David Walter	36	Indiana	County Clerk	Mud Springs Township.
Stucke, Jacob	39	Germany	Farmer	Mountain "
Sampson, Charles	26	England	Miner	Placerville "
Swanwell, Frederick	27	Denmark	Painter	" "
Shick, Michael	51	Maryland	Laborer	" "
Shattuck, Charles Wash	34	Pennsylvania	Teamster	" "
Schulmurch, Conrad	38	Germany	Miner	Coloma "
Stock, Wilson	36	Austria	Baker	" "
Short, Nelson	27	Michigan	Miner	Placerville "
Scott, John Gilbert	35	Ohio	Blacksmith	" "
Smith, James	71	Virginia	Pilot	" "
Slevin, Daniel	43	Ireland	Miner	" "
Sherwood, Benjamin	37	New York	Justice of Peace	" "
Shelton, Charles	36	Kentucky	Soldier	" "
Strong, DeWitt Clinton	42	New York	Miner	" "
Sprague, Eathan Allen	54	Maine	"	" "
Sloan, Thomas Jefferson	30	Ohio	Hotel-keeper	" "
Sturtevant, Stephen W	44	Maine	Carpenter	" "
Stephens, Hester	46	Pennsylvania	Farmer	" "
Starkey, John	74	Pennsylvania	Miner	Mud Springs "
Sims, Jacob Franklin	37	Ohio	"	Coloma "
Starrett, William	33	Maine	Farmer	Placerville "
Stetson, Alva Marshall	39	New York	Engineer	Kelsey "
Stanaway, Samuel	25	England	Mason	Diamond Sp'gs "
Scott, Thomas Beal	54	Virginia	Miner	Placerville "
Stout, Geo. Washington	46	Ohio	Hotel-keeper	" "
Smithhouse, Henry	32	Hanover	Miner	Dutch Bar "
Schweizer, Tobias	38	Switzerland	Blacksmith	Coloma "
Smith, Henry	27	Hesse Darmst.	Miner	Placerville "
Sullivan, John Joseph	28	Ireland	"	Latrobe.
Swartz, John	50	France	"	Placerville Township.

NAME.	Age	Place of Nativity.	Occupation.	Local Residence.
Simonton, Adam	31	Tennessee	Water Agent	Placerville Township.
Sexton, Wiley	32	Tennessee	Laborer	" "
Sweeney, James	35	Ireland	Farmer	Coloma "
Slesbuttel, Alexander	49	Hamburg	Hotel-keeper	Diamond Sp. "
Shea, John	34	Massachusetts	Laborer	Placerville "
Smiley, James	60	Pennsylvania	Farmer	Mud Springs "
Schooler, William Horton	47	Kentucky	Miner	Coloma "
Smith, Fidel	50	Germany	Farmer	Placerville "
Skinner, James, Sr	53	Scotland	"	White Oak "
Slater, George	53	England	"	Placerville "
Smith, Edwin Hurlburt	51	New York	"	" "
Scott, Michael	43	England	Miner	" "
Schmidt, John Frederick	34	Germany	Laborer	" "
Sealy, William	65	Massachusetts	Miner	" "
Stephens, Thomas	32	England	"	" "
Standeford, Wm. Walter	38	Indiana	Ditch Agent	Mud Springs "
Shank, Charles	47	Denmark	Farmer	" "
Smith, Ekin	44	England	"	" "
Simmons, Joseph Everett	36	Massachusetts	Miner	" "
Steffani, Serafin	38	Switzerland	Farmer	Kelsey "
Swift, Isaac Granall	27	Massachusetts	"	Greenwood "
Smith, Ezra Morton	31	Ohio	"	Coloma "
Shamel, Benjamin	49	Ohio	Miner	" "
Stow, Henry Kirk	38	Connecticut	Lawyer	" "
Storer, John Hassam	37	New York	Carpenter	" "
Shore, Richard	58	Kentucky	Farmer	Cosumnes "
Skidmore, James	57	Kentucky	"	" "
Seely, Nathias	38	Ohio	Miner	" "
Slaughter, John Wesley	32	Ohio	Ditch Agent	" "
Smith, William Calvin	20	North Carolina	Miner	" "
Sessor, James Sample	43	Ohio	Merchant	Placerville "
Shilling, Saul S.	24	Ohio	Clerk	" "
Spencer, Oscar Fitz Allen	24	Iowa	Farmer	" "
Swertcope, Jno. Valentine	55	New York	Miner	" "
Stephenson, Jacob Henry	35	Norway	"	Greenwood "
Schmidt, Joseph	42	France	"	" "
Sampson, John	40	Sweden	Farmer	Salmon Falls "
Stephens, Francis	38	Pennsylvania	Miner	Diamond Spr'gs "
Spooner, John Quincy	41	Vermont	Farmer	Mud Springs "
Schlaier, Gustave	32	Germany	Miner	Diamond Spr'gs "
Smith, Stearns Fisher	31	Ohio	"	" "
Slater, Edward	27	England	Teamster	Placerville "
Saxton, Geo. Washington	52	Massachusetts	Miner	" "
Sanders, Chancy	48	New York	Farmer	Mud Springs "
Smith, Joseph	41	New York	Miner	Salmon Falls "
Sheppard, Wm. George	37	Great Britain	Merchant	Pleasant Valley.
Stegall, Hensley	38	South Carolina	Farmer	Georgetown.
Steere, Robert	33	New York	Rev. Collector	Mud Springs "
Shepherd, Benj. Franklin	26	England	Merchant	Georgetown "
Scolari, Luigi	40	Switzerland	Farmer	Coloma "
Searles, Daniel	37	New York	"	" "
Stephens, T. Cadwallon	45	Wales	Watchmaker	Placerville "
Scott, Robert	41	Scotland	Miner	Mud Springs "
Stoffels, Nicholas	36	Prussia	Merchant	Jay Hawk.
Stone, William Hudson	50	Kentucky	Ditch Owner	Georgetown "
Smith, Andrew Jackson	32	Pennsylvania	Farmer	" "
Spencer, Willis Eugene	37	New York	Dentist	" "
Spencer, Henry	37	Vermont	Miner	" "
Swift, Joseph	63	Massachusetts	Farmer	" "
Sornberger, Harmon	28	New York	Miner	" "
Seyton, Isaac	50	Vermont	Cattle Drover	" "
Shattuck, Henry Clay	36	Illinois	Miner	" "
Slingerland, Henry	42	Pennsylvania	Mechanic	" "

NAME.	Age	Place of Nativity.	Occupation.	Local Residence.
Smith, James	29	Virginia	Teamster	Georgetown Township.
Smith, Martin	40	Pennsylvania	Agt. W.,F. &Co.	Strawberry Valley.
Spencer, Francis Newton	27	Missouri	Driver	" "
Smith, Ellicin	48	South Carolina	Farmer	Gold Hill.
Smith, Jordan Bales	61	Ohio	Miner	Kelsey Township.
Selby, William Henry	36	Maryland	"	" "
Stileler, William	70	Pennsylvania	"	" "
Safford, Shubad Anson	37	New York	Water Agent	Diamond Springs T'p.
Sheppard, James	51	Ohio	Miner	" " "
Savage, Mark Cook	36	Maine	"	" " "
Sheppard, Elisha White	33	Missouri	"	" " "
Saulsbury, Sam'l Duncan	46	New York	"	" " "
Small, Martin Van Buren	30	Maine	"	" " "
Steadman, Chris. Potter	63	Rhode Island	"	" " "
Shneider, John, Jr.	22	Illinois	Clerk	" " "
Smoyer, Charles	42	Pennsylvania	Miner	Cosumnes Township.
Scott, Ebenezer	60	New York	Farmer	" "
Stevenson, Virgil	48	Ohio	Laborer	" "
Staples, Charles	42	Missouri	Miner	" "
Smith, Sylvester Harvey	32	Pennsylvania	"	" "
Smith, Marshall	68	Maryland	"	" "
Southard, Lemuel	41	Virginia	"	" "
Seely, David Taylor	33	Ohio	"	" "
Soliss, Daniel Bleanoss	36	New York	"	" "
Spaulding, G. Washingt'n	37	Kentucky	"	" "
Stumpff, Lafayette	32	Kentucky	"	" "
Sutters, Samuel	43	Pennsylvania	"	" "
Stillwaggon, James	34	Pennsylvania	"	" "
Smith, James Henry	36	Connecticut	Clerk	Greenwood "
Stoel, Richard	29	New York	Miner	" "
Shepherd, Orl'o Edmerson	47	Ohio	"	" "
Savery, Hiram Nye	59	Massachusetts	"	" "
Shaffer, Levi Rice	36	Pennsylvania	Farmer	" "
Stiffler, Peter	52	Ohio	"	" "
Stephens, Samuel George	38	Georgia	Miner	" "
Sliger, James	40	Tennessee	"	" "
Sungfrank, Absolem	42	Ohio	"	" "
Simpers, Geo. Washing'n	38	Maryland	"	" "
Stoddard, Hiram	35	Massachusetts	Farmer	" "
Seymour, War'n Carlysle	33	Illinois	Miner	Mud Springs "
Salmon, John	39	Ohio	"	" "
Smith, Alonzo Ludlow	28	New York	Livery Stable	" "
Stilwell, Samuel Martin	48	New York	Butcher	" "
Smith, Edward Payson	26	Illinois	Shepherd	" "
Shrewsbury, L. Morris	36	Virginia	Constable	" "
Smith, Harvey	35	New York	Blacksmith	" "
Shrader, Jacob Christie	27	Ohio	Laborer	" "
Shirley, William Dearing	66	South Carolina	General Trader	" "
Shirley, Jack Breeze	26	Illinois	Laborer	" "
Steiner, James Frederick	27	Michigan	Farmer	" "
Shaver, James King	38	Tennessee	Trader	" "
Spencer, Charles	49	Pennsylvania	Miner	Placerville "
Smith, Samuel Augustus	45	Maryland	Justice of Peace	Kelsey "
Schaller, Christian	44	Germany	Miner	Greenwood "
Seifner, John	36	Prussia	"	Diamond Sp'gs "
Simson, Jorgen	46	Denmark	"	Salmon Falls "
Siesenop, August	43	Germany	"	Kelsey "
Shaver, Jacob	42	New York	Shoemaker	Mud Springs "
Stockman, John Lich	25	Ohio	Miner	Smith's Flat.
Schmidt, John	32	Bavaria	"	Diamond Springs T'p.
Smith, William	46	Sweden	Hose Maker	Placerville Township.
Skinner, John Dodd	48	Connecticut	Merchant	Kelsey "
Shepherd, John	42	Ohio	Carpenter	Diamond Spr. "

NAME.	Age	Place of Nativity.	Occupation.	Local Residence.
Summerfield, Jas. Wesley	42	Virginia	Farmer	Mud Springs Township.
Sperwer, William	42	Denmark	Miner	" " "
Souverign, Joshua	33	Canada	Carpenter	" " "
Self, Francis Travers	41	Missouri	Miner	Georgetown.
Shepard, Gilbert Dench	60	New York	Miner	Georgetown Township.
Smith, William	35	Ireland	"	Kelsey "
Smith, Calvin	62	New York	Farmer	Mud Springs "
Saulin, Andro	32	Austria	Miner	Placerville "
Smith, William	35	Great Britain	"	Kelsey "
Stearns, Leopold	40	Bohemia	Merchant	" "
Silva, Frank	36	Portugal	Teamster	Georgetown "
Stanton, Patrick	32	Ireland	Miner	" "
Swarz, Daniel	34	Bavaria	Baker	" "
Sampter, Henry	40	Prussia	Merchant	" "
Stahlman, William	40	Germany	Barber	" "
Smith, Thomas	39	Ireland	Miner	Greenwood "
Smith, John	28	Ireland	"	" "
Snider, Gottfried	26	Germany	Butcher	" "
Sherwood, John Dodson	30	Ohio	Miner	Salmon Falls "
Shields, Michael	29	Ireland	Teamster	Coloma "
Schmidt, Martin Paulsen	39	Denmark	Farmer	" "
Seegar, David	33	Hanover	Baker	" "
Stronach, Alexander	39	Scotland	Miner	" "
Stotter, John Henry	43	Denmark	Farmer	" "
Schlicher, George	66	Germany	Miner	" "
Schlicher, Henry	33	Germany	"	" "
Seely, Frank	38	France	Gardener	" "
Steffen, Peter	32	Prussia	Teamster	" "
Stuckslauger, Johnston R.	37	Pennsylvania	Miner	" "
Stolari, John	41	Switzerland	Farmer	" "
Smith, Moses Augustus	30	Virginia	Miner	White Oak "
Scheffbower, John	40	Germany	Farmer	" " "
Skinner, William	22	Massachusetts	Miner	" " "
Stellges, George	43	Hanover	"	" " "
Sherwood, Francis W	61	New York	"	Salmon Falls "
Stegeman, John	51	Holland	Farmer	" " "
Smith, Gerrard Diken	42	New York	Miner	" " "
Silberhorn, Chas. Theo	46	France	"	" " "
Spillane, Dennis	48	Ireland	"	" " "
Schwalm, Francis	42	France	Farmer	White Oak "
Shinn, James Madison	42	Ohio	Miner	Mud Springs "
Simas, Manuel	40	Portugal	Farmer	" " "
Stringham, Clark	33	New York	Stage Driver	" " "
Smith, Edward	38	North Carolina	Miner	" " "
Simpson, James	30	Scotland	Saloon-keeper	" " "
Schlotyhoner, Paul	40	Germany	Bakery	" " "
Spillane, Morris	34	Ireland	Miner	" " "
Storer, Moses Jackson	43	Massachusetts	Blacksmith	" " "
Stare, Samuel	57	Pennsylvania	Carpenter	Mountain "
Springer, Simon Boliver	36	New York	Farmer	" "
Smiley, Jeremiah Edward	35	Maine	Carpenter	" "
Sarvent, Thos. Jefferson	34	New York	Blacksmith	" "
Shrader, Henry	29	Hanover	Saloon-keeper	Cosumnes "
Stenger, John	40	Hesse Darmst.	Miner	" "
Smith, Jacob	36	Bavaria	"	" "
Scott, James	53	Scotland	Farmer	" "
Steiner, John	39	Bavaria	"	" "
Smith, Joseph Rafell	33	New Mexico	Miner	Diamond Springs "
Smith, Gilman Kendall	23	Illinois	Dairyman	" " "
Snow, Samuel Suisman	49	Prussia	Farmer	" " "
Schantz, Anthony	54	Germany	Miner	Clarksville.
Stonebreaker, Frederick	41	Prussia	Merchant	Georgetown Township.
Sehlmeyer, Henry Phillip	23	Hanover	Teamster	Mud Springs "

NAMES.	Age	Place of Nativity.	Occupation.	Local Residence.
Sinder, Louis	37	Hesse Cassell	Painter	Georgetown Township.
Sweeny, Michael	26	Great Britain	Miner	Coloma "
Smith, Thomas Pearce	41	Great Britain	Shoemaker	Mud Springs "
Saur, Conrad	39	Bavaria	Miner	Placerville "
Shetts, Henry	36	Ohio	Butcher	Diamond Sp'gs "
Scheff, Peter	39	France	Blacksmith	" "
Schlegel, Gustave	39	Germany	Farmer	Mud Springs "
Schmidt, Franz August	54	Hamburg	"	Diamond Spr'gs "
Seisbuttel, D. C. Buhring	41	Germany	Machinist	" "
Schanke, William	48	Germany	Shoemaker	" "
Schneider, John Sr	54	France	Farmer	" "
Sebastian, John	41	Bavaria	Miner	" "
Schaub, Joseph	65	France	Farmer	" "
Short, John Euing	30	Kentucky	Hostler	" "
Sexton, George Philip	37	Massachusetts	Miner	" "
Skinner, James	27	Scotland	Teamster	White Oak.
Shippy, Jonathan	46	Ohio	Miner	Grizzly Flat.
Schanz, Nicholas	48	Prussia	"	Diamond Springs.
Schalhaiser, Peter	52	France	"	" "
Swansborough, James	23	Wales	"	Placerville Township.
Steen, Isaac Marshall	37	Kentucky	"	Kelsey "
Smith, James	32	Great Britain	"	Placerville "
Slater, Thomas	47	Great Britain	"	" "
Stewart, Abraham	47	Great Britain	"	" "
Sublette, Alexander	28	Kentucky	Farmer	" "
Short, George Lemon	44	New York	Laborer	" "
Sumpti, Lewis	50	Prussia	Merchant	Georgetown "
Smith, Jacob	32	Baden	Brewer	Coloma "
Smith, John	40	Prussia	Miner	Greenwood "
Scott, Alexander	35	Denmark	"	Coloma "
Selleck, Luman	67	Vermont	Farmer	Placerville "
Smith, Foster Gaddis	27	Illinois	Lumberman	" "
Stevens, John Howland	44	New York	Butcher	" "
Stehley, Roman	44	Germany	Laborer	Coloma "
Sinclair, William	35	Ireland	Clerk	Latrobe.
Stroh, John	40	Prussia	Farmer	Coloma Township.
Saul, Charles	40	Ireland	Miner	Placerville "
Smith, James	30	Virginia	"	Georgetown "
Sites, Lewis	37	Ohio	"	" "
Shoemaker, Dan. Freeman	33	New York	"	" "
Snyder, Thomas Jefferson	36	Pennsylvania	"	" "
Staten, Nathan	36	Kentucky	"	" "
Snow, William Coonds	57	Maine	"	" "
Scott, James Riley	36	Kentucky	Farmer	Diamond Sp'gs "
Southwick, Hiram	36	New York	Miner	" "
Shearer, George	48	Pennsylvania	"	" "
Slack, Cornelius	40	New York	Farmer	" "
Sackett, Herman "S"	42	New York	Teamster	" "
St. Clair, John	31	Ohio	"	" "
Self, Green Berry	31	Tennessee	"	" "
Steele, Jackson Parker	30	Alabama	Farmer	" "
Stapleton, Thomas	35	New York	Miner	" "
Scott, David	32	Kentucky	Farmer	" "
Scott, George Washington	48	Pennsylvania	Miner	Placerville "
Smith, Levi	43	Massachusetts	Farmer	Coloma "
Smith, Dorman	46	Vermont	Miner	" "
Simmons, Jeradiah	43	Maine	"	" "
Simmons, James Peas	25	Maine	"	" "
Stevens, Stanford	57	Missouri	"	" "
Sheriff, Alfred Ross	32	Dis't Columbia	Wagon-maker	" "
Smith, William Nelson	40	New York	Minister	" "
Simmons, Henry Franklin	31	Massachusetts	Miner	El Dorado.
Sherwood, William Clark	41	New York	Farmer	Coloma Township.

NAMES.	Age	Place of Nativity.	Occupation.	Local Residence.
Snider, John	35	Pennsylvania	Miner	Nashville Township.
Scarborough, William	39	Georgia	"	Diamond Springs T'p.
Swendt, Randolph W. H.	36	New York	Carpenter	El Dorado.
Snellson, Spruce	38	Tennessee	Miner	Fair Play.
Sherbondy, John	34	Ohio	"	Cosumnes Township.
Smith, Thomas Jefferson	26	Illinois	"	" "
Stickney, Edson William	36	Ohio	"	" "
Starkey, Austin Morgan	35	Kentucky	Farmer	" "
Showers, William	41	Ohio	"	Placerville "
Sparks, Samuel Shrieves	36	Pennsylvania	Carpenter	White Oak "
Smith, Benjamin Buel	48	New York	Miner	Kelsey
Stahl, Joseph	34	Ohio	"	" "
Sevey, Thomas	39	New York	"	" "
Scott, John	49	England	"	Placerville "
Springer, Albert H. Alex.	45	Prussia	Vine-grower	Diamond Sp. "
Stroup, Henry	36	Michigan	Teamster	Placerville "
Spencer, Lorenzo	55	N. Hampshire	Farmer	" "
Steely, John	29	Missouri	Miner	" "
Smith, Anthony	34	Tennessee	Teamster	" "
Stone, Wm. H. Harrison	26	Michigan	"	" "
Scott, Robinson Cyrus	33	Indiana	Miner	" "
Stewart, John Milton	37	Vermont	"	Mountain "
Shivel, Noah Demming	36	Ohio	"	" "
Stockdale, David Finley	32	Ohio	"	" "
Sperbeck, And. Jackson	28	New York	"	" "
Steele, James Newton	38	Indiana	"	Kelsey "
Stewart, John	50	Scotland	"	Coloma "
Serber, Jerrmirah	37	Kentucky	Ditch Agent	Georgetown "
Spencer, Patrick Henry	38	Vermont	Miner	" "
Shoemaker, Daniel F.	34	New York	"	" "
Sizer, George	45	New York	Farmer	Diamond Sp. "
Sheridan, Thomas	31	New York	Teamster	" "
Schofield, Charles W.	40	New York	Laborer	Placerville "
Shepard, Levi	38	New York	Miner	" "
Sibeck, Charles	30	New York	Lumberman	Diamond Sp. "
Shorey, Albert	30	Maine	Hostler	Placerville "
Smith, Henry	36	Hanover	Miner	Kelsey "
Smith, Philip	38	Darmstadt	"	Placerville "
Smith, Geo. Washington	40	Maryland	"	" "
Smith, John Louis	53	Pennsylvania	"	Salmon Falls "
Spinks, Charles	45	England	"	Mud Springs "
Schneider, Henry	33	Switzerland	Butcher	Pleasant Valley.
Sharp, James	37	Canada	Miner	Placerville Township.
Seweryn, Gorski	36	Poland	"	Mud Springs "
Southleng, Gustave	47	Sweden	Carpenter	Uniontown. "
Swap, Henry	44	Bavaria	Farmer	Salmon Falls "
Sherburne, John Leonard	25	Maine	Miner	Georgetown.
Smith, John Farnham	46	Maine	Laborer	Lake Valley.
Simmons, Joel	39	Maine	Miner	Gold Hill.
Smith, Humph'y Hathway	27	Massachusetts	Laborer	Cold Springs.
Stratton, Jason Nathaniel	37	Massachusetts	Miner	Greenwood Township.
Stewart, Nelson	43	Ohio	"	" "
Smith, Jacob Lawrence	21	Illinois	"	Placerville "
Short, Amasa	58	New York	"	" "
Sumrow, Henry	39	North Carolina	"	Mud Springs "
Smith, Hugh R	41	Ohio	"	Mountain "
Shaw, George Haley	28	Maine	Teleg'h ope'tor	Shingle Sp'gs "
Sturgill, James George	39	North Carolina	Blacksmith	Latrobe.
Scott, William Burton	36	Delaware	Farmer	Shingle Springs.
Stiles, Richard Norton	50	New Jersey	Miner	El Dorado.
Smith, John Richardson	40	New York	Laborer	Latrobe.
Sprigg, Zachariah Dorsey	48	Kentucky	Carpenter	El Dorado.
Saul, Albert Manning	33	Ireland	Hotel-keeper	Smith's Flat.

NAME.	Age	Place of Nativity.	Occupation.	Local Residence.
Sexton, Michael	26	Ireland	Water Agent	Placerville Township.
Swasey, Joseph	39	Portugal	Miner	Georgetown "
Saroney, Augustus	36	New York	"	White Oak "
Sweezey, Hiram	30	New York	Lumberman	Placerville "
Stone, William Henry	27	Michigan	Hostler	" "
Shane, Valentine	40	Germany		Cosumnes "
Smith, Jonathan Pickrel	35	Ohio	Teamster	Georgetown "
Sexton, John	30	Ireland	Stone mason	Placerville "
Stroup, Lewis Thomas	50	Delaware	Farmer	Salmon Falls "
Sobrenzen, Hennrich	38	Denmark	Miner	Greenwood "
Spickert, Jacob	42	Bavaria	Shoemaker	Placerville "
Searfoss, Jacob	47	Pennsylvania	Carpenter	" "
Stone, George Washingt'n	24	Michigan	Stage Driver	" "
Stanley, John	51	England	Miner	Diamond Spr'gs "
Silvas, Antone	46	Portugal	Farmer	Greenwood "
Sarter, Joseph William	34	Switzerland	Butcher	Georgetown "
Sybert, John Henry	36	New York	Miner	Greenwood "
Sattler, Bernhard	32	Baden	"	Diamond Spr'gs "

T

NAME.	Age	Place of Nativity.	Occupation.	Local Residence.
Tong, Gilbert Shores	35	Missouri	Carpenter	White Oak Township.
Tong, Samuel	38	Missouri	Farmer	" "
Taylor, Hugh Brotherton	40	Pennsylvania	"	" "
Tobey, James Marion	31	Massachusetts	Miner	" "
Truitt, James "R"	37	Kentucky	Farmer	" "
Theison, John	34	Luxemburg	Brewer	Mud Springs "
Turman, Hosea Bent	29	Illinois	Printer	Placerville "
Tagtmeir, Frederick	30	Prussia	Musician	" "
Tew, Calvin Smith	40	Ohio	Miner	Coloma "
Titus, Isaac Sutthen	38	New York	Physician	Placerville "
Trotter, Robert	50	Ireland	Miner	Georgetown "
True, Charles Frederick	23	Maine	Teacher	Greenwood "
Taft, Pliny Merrick	36	Massachusetts	Miner	Placerville "
Teuscher, John	43	Bavaria	Cooper	Coloma "
Tripp, Henry Orton	43	New York	Miner	Placerville "
Titler, Elisha Jackson	37	Ohio	"	" "
Turman, Benjamin Isaac	23	Illinois	Clerk	" "
Thompson, George Henry	46	Ohio	Miner	" "
Tucker, Daniel Shell	47	Virginia	"	" "
Tracy, Henry Numbers	29	Ohio	Shoemaker	" "
Tryon, Ambrose Bruen	34	New Jersey	Cabinet-maker	" "
Trask, William Wallace	40	Pennsylvania	Farmer	" "
Tinney, Henry John	35	England	"	Coloma "
Tingle, James	32	Kentucky	Miner	Placerville "
Towns, Charles	53	New York	Farmer	" "
Towns, Franklin	25	New York	"	" "
Taylor, Oscar Morehouse	48	Vermont	Horticulturist	" "
Toombs, William	42	England	Miner	" "
Taylor, George	39	England	"	Greenwood "
Taylor, Noah Columbus	43	South Carolina	Physician	Mud Springs "
Trescott, Joseph Carlton	37	Vermont	Stage propriet'r	Coloma "
Tarr, Jonathan	28	Maine	Lumberman	Cosumnes "
Tryon, Charles Edwin	36	New Jersey	Blacksmith	Placerville "
Tutchlaff, Louis	27	Prussia	Farmer	Kelsey "
Taylor, William Harrison	47	Massachusetts	Physician	Coloma "
Tocini, Giovani	23	Italy	Miner	Newtown.
Tipton, Hiram	36	Pennsylvania	"	Kelsey Township.
Turner, Jacob Perry	46	Pennsylvania	Millwright	Diamond Spr'gs "
Tripp, William Franklin	40	Massachusetts	Carpenter	Placerville "
Taylor, Samuel	35	Pennsylvania	Clerk	Georgetown "
Thurston, Eugen True	39	Maine	School Teacher	" "
Tagart, John	42	Missouri	Laborer	Lake Valley "

NAMES.	Age	Place of Nativity.	Occupation.	Local Residence.
Titler, John Martin	30	Ohio	Miner	Strawberry.
Triplett, Liberty Major P.	40	Kentucky	"	Coloma Township.
Tullar, Alvin Hyde	48	Vermont	Road Overseer	Salmon Falls Township.
Thompson, Ebenezer	32	New York	Miner	Kelsey "
Tucker, Joseph Wood	39	Massachusetts	Merchant	" "
Tanner, William Madison	54	Kentucky	Farmer	Diamond Springs "
Turner, Ezra	50	New York	Lumberman	" " "
Tingley, Samuel	37	Ohio	Miner	" " "
Twitchell, Asa Cousins	49	Maine	Farmer	" " "
Taylor, Jonathan	65	Virginia	Butcher	Cosumnes "
Tarr, Daniel	40	Maine	Lumberman	" "
Tarr, Jefferson	36	Maine	"	" "
Tyler, Benjamin Small	44	Maine	"	" "
Tyler, Adam Brid	27	Maine	Laborer	" "
Taylor, Edward Tyffe	30	Ohio	Butcher	" "
Terry, Isiah Eldridge	34	Massachusetts	Miner	Greenwood "
Thompson, Hugh Paden	36	New York	"	" "
Taylor, Noah Columbus	42	South Carolina	Physician	Shingle Springs.
Tracy, Horace Franklin	39	Vermont	Farmer	Aurum City.
Titus, Samuel Jones	47	Pennsylvania	Miner	Kelsey Township.
Tooker, Lansing	66	New York	Teacher	Placerville Township.
Taylor, William	50	England	Farmer	Greenwood "
Truitt, Austin	41	Indiana	Miner	Placerville "
Trotot, Nicholas	54	France	Farmer	Diamond Sp'gs "
Tanner, George	33	Nova Scotia	Carpenter	Kelsey "
Taylor, Solomon	68	Georgia	Miner	Georgetown "
Thompson, Joseph	40	England	"	" "
Trimble, William	36	Pennsylvania	Farmer	" "
Thrasher, Stephen Perry	38	Missouri	Miner	" "
Taylor, Curtis	39	New York	"	Greenwood.
Trimble, George	55	Ireland	Farmer	Coloma Township.
Teuscher, Daniel	32	Bavaria	Miner	" "
Teuscher, Phillip	39	Bavaria	"	" "
Torrance, Merrit Herd	32	New York	"	White Oak Township.
Thomas, William	55	Connecticut	Farmer	" " "
Taylor, John Thompson	34	Kentucky	Miner	Salmon Falls "
Thompson, Peter Madison	44	Denmark	Clerk	White Oak "
Tune, John Hill	45	Virginia	Miner	Salmon Falls "
Turneman, Oswald D. R.	37	Sweden	Farmer	" " "
Treuholtz, Ernst Magnus	46	Prussia	Physician	Mud Springs "
Taylor, Joseph	63	Kentucky	Farmer	" " "
Theiss, Charles Henry	27	Germany	Saloon-keeper	" " "
Thompson, Thomas Ruel	33	Maine	Road Overseer	Cosumnes "
Tholen, Harmon Henry	38	Germany	Miner	" "
Thaten, Jacob Andreas	35	England	"	Coloma "
Thompson, Conrad	50	Sweden	"	Greenwood "
Thomas, Abraham C	51	Kentucky	"	Mud Springs "
Tynan, Timothy	55	Great Britain	"	Diamond Springs "
Theisen, Nicholas	40	Germany	Farmer	" " "
Thatcher, Wm. Wallace	34	Ohio	Hotel-keeper	Placerville "
Turnbull, Robert Oliver	26	Canada	Merchant	" "
Tomlinson, Jacob H	43	Pennsylvania	Miner	" "
Taggart, William	69	Ohio	Manufacturer	" "
Taylor, Robert jr	36	Pennsylvania	Teacher	Kelsey "
Tekemeyer, Frederick	48	Prussia	Miner	Diamond Springs "
Trunk, Frank	40	Bavaria	Farmer	Greenwood "
Tusdale, Thomas	32	Scotland	Ditch Agent	Diamond Springs "
Theison, Jacob	55	Germany	Farmer	" " "
Thompkins, Herman	33	New York	Miner	Greenwood "
Taggert, James	71	Pennsylvania	"	Placerville "
Thomas, John Franklin	38	Georgia	Merchant	Georgetown "
Thompson, John M	36	Virginia	Miner	" "
Taylor, Frank	25	Illinois	"	Diamond Springs "

NAME.	Age	Place of Nativity.	Occupation.	Local Residence.
Tillman, William	36	Ohio	Teamster	Diamond Springs T'p.
Tew, William Henry	26	Ohio	Miner	Coloma "
Troyman, Reuben	40	Virginia	"	" "
Tyler, Richard John	47	Virginia	"	" "
Tyler, William	33	Kentucky	"	El Dorado.
Thompson, John	45	Virginia	"	Shingle Springs.
Taylor, William Thornton	30	Virginia	"	El Dorado.
Tyler, Thadeus	39	South Carolina	Teamster	Shingle Springs.
Terry, Orlando	29	Pennsylvania	Miner	" "
Thatcher, John Saford	24	New York	Teamster	Cosumnes Township.
Tong, William Richard	22	Missouri	"	White Oak "
Tillinghast, John William	45	Rhode Island	Miner	Greenwood "
Thomas, John Wilson	45	Connecticut	Stage driver	Shingle Springs.
Torrence, Milton	59	North Carolina	Miner	Georgetown Township.
Thomas, Alexande Geo	35	North Carolina	"	" "
Trickey, Zephaniah Miller	45	New York	"	Diamond Sp'gs "
Tindell, Samuel Hennger	40	Tennessee	Farmer	Placerville "
Tuers, Abraham	64	New York	"	Diamond Sp'gs "
Turbach, Christian	38	Prussia	Miner	Placerville "
Tripp, Stephen Rodman	37	Massachusetts	Farmer	" "
Townsend, Almun Abrose	31	New York	Teamster	" "
Taylor, Alvin	35	Pennsylvania	Farmer	El Dorado "
Taylor, George William	29	Indiana	"	Latrobe.
Tripp, Stephen Rodman	28	Rhode Island	Miner	El Dorado.
True, Isaac Richard	24	Ohio	Teamster	Shingle Springs.
Tisdale, Franklin	24	Missouri	Laborer	Latrobe.
Thomas, Herbert	42	England	Hotel keeper	Placerville Township.
Tuch, John	55	Holland	Teamster	Salmon Falls "
Thatcher, Jacob Ernest	26	Ohio	"	Placerville "
Tarney, James	21	New York	Landlord	" "
Tipswood, Abert	25	Illinois	Miner	" "
Thome, Mathias	29	Germany	Farmer	" "
Teachert, John Charles	28	Germany	Miner	Greenwood "
Taylor, Orson Augustus	36	Vermont	Stock driver	Coloma "
Tompkins, Charles	39	Great Britain	Miner	" "
Taylor, James	68	Tennessee	Farmer	Placerville "
Taylor, Joseph	39	Ireland	Ditch Agent	" "
Tarry, Homer Francis	27	New York	Laborer	Greenwood "

U

NAME.	Age	Place of Nativity.	Occupation.	Local Residence.
Utz, Lytle Wiley	39	Indiana	Miner	White Oak Township.
Uhlenkamp, Martnus	47	Germany	Carpenter	" "
Uhlenkamp, Conrad	42	Germany	Cabinet-maker	" "
Ury, Jacob	32	Ohio	Miner	Georgetown "
Ubldin, William Miller	30	Wisconsin	"	Fair Play.
Upton, Franklin	37	Massachusetts	Carpenter	Placerville Township.
Utt, Lysander	42	Virginia	Farmer	Pilot Hill.
Underwood, Ira Amos	24	New York	Miner	Mud Springs.

V

NAME.	Age	Place of Nativity.	Occupation.	Local Residence.
Vickry, Abner George	35	Georgia	Miner	White Oak Township.
Vanderhayden, John Gee	44	New York	Saloon-keeper	Coloma "
Vernon, William Patrick	39	Tennessee	Farmer	" "
Veerkamp, Francis	43	Germany	"	" "
Vantine, John	33	New York	Barber	Placerville "
Vincent, Samuel	26	England	Miner	" "
Van Vleck, Amos	49	New York	Farmer	" "
Varozzo, Moreo	23	Switzerland	Dairyman	" "
Van Voorhies, Ralph Jos'h	24	Michigan	Druggist	" "
Van Voorhies, Albert Alex	32	New Jersey	Saddler	" "
Vineyard, Geo. Wash'ton	34	Missouri	Miner	" "

NAME.	Age	Place of Nativity.	Occupation.	Local Residence.
Van Voorhies, Henry	27	New Jersey	Saddler	Placerville Township.
Veatch, John Alfred	24	Texas	Miner	" "
Venables, George Wm.	28	Connecticut	Teamster	Diamond Springs.
Valentine, William Henry	35	New York	Ditch Agent	Uniontown.
Vanderveer, Isaac	66	New York	Miner	Kelsey Township.
Van Horn, Sylvester	39	New York	Lumberman	Diamond Springs.
Votaw, Silas Philip	42	Missouri	Farmer	Coyoteville.
Vose, John Gilbert	27	Maine	"	"
Van Namee, Hiram Moe.	45	New York	"	Greenwood Township.
Vaughn, George Leonard	43	New York	"	Mud Springs "
Verrinder, George	30	New York	"	" "
Vesso, John Peter	65	France	Miner	Greenwood "
Von Bramen, Henrich	31	Bremen	"	" "
Vertmeyer, Edward	45	Hanover	"	" "
Vance, Enos	27	Illinois	Shinglemaker	Placerville "
Vannice, Cornelius	58	Ohio	Miner	" "
Vittle William	43	Great Britain	Farmer	Mud Springs
Veutich, Nicola	31	Austria	Miner	Placerville "
Vannine, Alexander	24	Switzerland	Restaurant	" "
Vande, Plas Louis	44	Belgium	Miner	Kelsey "
Vaughn, John	30	Illinois	"	Georgetown "
Vaughn, Wm. Hansford	34	Illinois	"	" "
Vancil, John William	26	Illinois	"	El Dorado.
Ventres, Noah Clark	51	Connecticut	"	Kelsey Township.
Vancamp, Abraham Bird	36	Pennsylvania	Farmer	Greenwood "
Van Martin, John Milton	27	Ohio	Engineer	Grizzly Flat.
Vandergriff, Gib	40	Tennessee	Miner	Salmon Falls.
Vance, James	50	Ohio	Teamster	Placerville,
Vineyard, James Russell	28	Wisconsin	Carpenter	El Dorado.

W

NAME.	Age	Place of Nativity.	Occupation.	Local Residence.
Williams, Sherrod	61	Kentucky	Lawyer	Placerville Township.
Whitney, John Osborn	45	Massachusetts	Miner	Clarkesville "
Winchell, Franklin Fay'te	58	New York	Farmer	" "
Winchell, Charles Perry	21	Illinois	Miner	" "
Willetts, William "H"	50	New York	Farmer	White Oak "
Warren, George Martin	51	Virginia	Miner	" "
Wishart, William	45	New York	"	" "
Wittenberg, Frederick	28	Indiana	"	" "
Waymouth, Jas. Lambert	39	Virginia	Saloon-keeper	Placerville "
Worthen, H. Wm. Austin	48	Virginia	Physician	" "
Wickman, Theodore	42	Hanover	Hotel-keeper	" "
White, Robert	39	Great Britain	Druggist	" "
Wilson, Jeptha	32	Missouri	Miner	Salmon Falls "
Wald, Julius	29	Denmark	"	White Oak "
Woods, Samuel Noyes	54	Vermont	Teamster	Placerville "
Wing, Samuel Spear	29	Maine	Miner	" "
Waller, Richard Franklin	35	Missouri	Wood Dealer	Latrobe.
Wickes, Alex. Mackey	37	New York	Teamster	Placerville Township.
Woodruff, Albert	33	Connecticut	Merchant	Coloma "
Weatheril, William	68	England	Engraver	Placerville "
Wiley, Timothy	45	Massachusetts	Laborer	" "
Wonderly, John Peters	36	Pennsylvania	Carpenter	" "
Willing, Robert Nichols	36	England	Merchant	Shingle Springs.
Webb, John Simpson	45	Virginia	Miner	Kelsey Township.
Warren, Geo. Augustus	42	Maine	Livery	Placerville "
Walls, John	34	Pennsylvania	Speculator	" "
Ward, Anthony	40	Ireland	Teamster	" "
Weyman, William	28	Illinois	Miner	" "
White, Joseph	45	Pennsylvania	"	" "
Willets, Stephen	46	New York	"	" "
Wulle, Joseph	33	Germany	"	Coloma "

NAMES.	Age	Place of Nativity.	Occupation.	Local Residence.
Wagner, Andrew	51	Germany	Blacksmith	White Oak Township.
Wanneumacher, Ruphert.	32	Germany	Brewer	Placerville "
Wattles, Charles Hodley..	41	Connecticut	Joiner	Kelsey "
White, Marshal	38	Illinois	Farmer	Placerville "
Watson, John Fletcher	51	Vermont	Miner	" "
Williams, Benj. S. Edge'n	41	Vermont	Carpenter	" "
Wolf, James	46	Ohio	Miner	" "
Williams, George Erwin..	28	Kentucky	Dist. Attorney..	" "
Wallace, Samuel	61	New York	Stone mason	" "
Walker, William James...	26	Ohio	Miner	" "
Waters, John	39	England	"	" "
Walf, Henry	37	Hanover	Farmer	White Oak.
Wright, Wm. Whitcomb..	44	N. Hampshire..	Carpenter	Placerville Township.
Wasson, George Augustus	40	New York	Water Agent	Diamond Spr'gs "
Wilcox, Truman	42	New York	Merchant	Placerville "
Watson, Jacob	41	Wisconsin	Miner	White Oak "
Williamson, Wm. Macaltr'e	49	Ohio	"	Placerville "
Welch, Michael	45	Ireland	Teamster	" "
Weber, Ernst	40	Saxony	Miner	" "
Wasson, Caldwell	41	New York	Farmer	Coloma "
Weaver, Harrison	36	Kentucky	Miner	Placerville "
Williams, David Henry....	29	Wales	Ditch Agent	" "
Weber, Christian	40	Holland	Tailor	" "
Weaver, Samuel	31	Scotland	Farmer	" "
Ward, Joseph	31	England	Laborer	" "
Wetherwax, J. M. Bowers	54	New York	Farmer	Mud Springs "
Wilson, John	44	England	Miner	White Oak "
Worden, James Barculo..	35	New York	"	Greenwood "
Wynkoop, Everet	44	New York	"	Coloma "
Wixom, Percival P	35	Michigan	Farmer	" "
Weller, Elias	33	Ohio	Merchant	" "
Welsh, William	74	North Carolina	Miner	Placerville "
Wickham, Daniel Clay	42	New York	Engineer	" "
Wait, George	43	New York	Hotel keeper	" "
Weaver, Benj. Franklin...	32	New York	Tailor	" "
Weatherwax, Chas. Henry	26	Michigan	Tinsmith	" "
Washburn, Lafayette	37	New York	Farmer	Diamond Spr'gs "
White, George	30	England	Teamster	Mud Springs "
Washburn, Marcus	34	New York	Lumberman	Diamond Spr'gs "
Weissner, John	48	Germany	Farmer	Mud Springs "
Worthing, Alfred Marshall	36	Maine	Blacksmith	Placerville "
Warriner, Samuel Miller..	45	New York	Farmer	Diamond Spr'gs "
Watson, Elijah Harper	53	Mississippi	Miner	Georgetown "
Williams, Crockett	31	Tennessee	"	" "
Woodside, Milton Alexan'r	45	North Carolina	"	" "
Williams, Eli	38	New York	Tailor	" "
Wait, Hiram	39	New York	Miner	" "
Wade, David Alexander...	42	South Carolina	"	" "
Williams, Russell	63	Georgia	"	" "
Waldo, Anson	37	Ohio	Farmer	" "
Werntz, Gabriel	32	Pennsylvania..	Blacksmith	Lake Valley "
Watson, Charles	38	New York	Landlord	" "
Washeim, Charles	22	Pennsylvania	Operator	" "
William, William Todd...	52	New Jersey	Driver	" "
Wood, William	50	New York	Farmer	Kelsey "
Wind, Lewis	34	Pennsylvania	"	" "
Wilkins, Chas. Granville..	44	N. Hampshire..	"	" "
Wooster, George Wheeler	36	Connecticut	"	" "
White, Josiah	42	Virginia	Carpenter	" "
Walls, Andrew	36	Missouri	Miner	Cosumnes "
Wheeler, Stephen Clark..	37	Indiana	Machinist	" "
White, Isaac Liver	60	Massachusetts	Miner	" "
Wilson, Horace	29	New York	Farmer	" "

NAME.	Age	Place of Nativity.	Occupation.	Local Residence.
Wistfall, Henry Harper	40	Virginia	Miner	Cosumnes Township,
Wetherbee, George W	31	Maine	"	" "
Wade, John	34	Indiana	"	Greenwood "
Wise, John Francis	32	New York	"	" "
Wilson, James St. Clair	30	Tennessee	"	" "
Willow, Elias	41	Pennsylvania	Merchant	El Dorado.
Woolery, Silas	49	Kentucky	Farmer	Mud Springs Township
Woolery, Harvey Jeffers'n	24	Missouri	"	" " "
Wilder, Benj. Wilkinson	45	Rhode Island	Miner	" " "
Warf, Andrew Jackson	33	Georgia	"	" " "
Watkins, David	48	Ohio	Farmer	" " "
Walker, Samuel Newell	42	Indiana	Miner	" " "
Wilcox, DeWitt Clinton	39	New York	Saloon-keeper	" " "
Warren, Francis Pierce	62	New York	Wheelwright	" " "
Winkleman, Jacob	61	Switzerland	Brewer	Greenwood "
Wings, James	40	England	Road Overseer	White Oak "
Wible, Simon William	35	Pennsylvania	Miner	Mud Springs "
Walk, John Wilbirn	33	North Carolina	Teamster	Diamond Spr'gs "
Winkleman, Jacob, Jr	36	Switzerland	Hotel-keeper	Greenwood "
Waggner, Phillip	39	Bavaria	Baker	" "
Williamson, James	27	Iowa	Miner	Placerville "
Ward, Thomas	37	England	"	" "
Ward, Robert	34	England	"	" "
Ward, John	39	England	"	Kelsey "
Woodford, Elias	40	Connecticut	"	Coloma "
Wintermantel, Anthony	40	Germany	Farmer	Coloma "
Weston, Samuel Truant	46	Maine	"	Mud Springs "
Wallace, Charles Clark	34	New York	Clergyman	Placerville "
White, William	35	Ireland	Farmer	Coloma "
Weinking, Henry	41	Germany	Miner	Greenwood "
Wiley, Rheuben Rich	44	Maine	"	Georgetown "
White, Joseph Fullerton	50	Pennsylvania	"	" "
Webster, Daniel Clough	42	N. Hampshire	"	" "
Walk, John Franklin	49	North Carolina	"	Diamond Springs.
Wells, John Rodneld	40	Brazil	"	Kelsey Township.
Weber, Peter	58	Prussia	"	" "
Wolf, Phillip	54	Germany	"	" "
Waldeck, Heinrich	34	Elec. of H. Cas	"	" "
White, Jonathan Breck	40	Maine	"	Georgetown Township
Williams, John	35	Great Britain	"	" "
Whiteside, Joseph	31	Scotland	"	" "
Ward, Robert Garret	52	New York	Blacksmith	" "
Wagner, John Westley	40	Pennsylvania	Miner	" "
Wurges, Jacob	45	Nassau	"	Greenwood "
Wise, Phillip	40	Wirtemburg	"	" "
Wurges, William	44	Nassau	"	" "
Webber, George	34	Newfoundland	"	" "
Wintermantel, Louis	42	Baden	Farmer	Coloma "
Wanzer, John William	24	Iowa	"	White Oak "
Weber, Charles	33	Prussia	Miner	" " "
White, Benjamin	63	New York	Farmer	" " "
Wubbena, Garrit Mensen	43	Hanover	"	Salmon Falls "
Wardwell, Jairus V	35	Maine	Manuf. of Lime	" " "
Welling, Leonard	35	Germany	Farmer	" " "
Wilson, William	69	Scotland	Miner	White Oak "
Wendin, John	36	Sweden	"	Mud Springs "
Wallin, Jonas	39	Sweden	Farmer	White Oak "
West, Franklin	37	Denmark	"	Mud Springs "
Wheeler, George	37	Maine	Miner	Mountain "
Wheeler, Moses Chandler	34	Maine	"	" "
Wahner, Valentine	38	Germany	Shoemaker	" "
Wall, Benjamin Franklin	46	England	Miner	Cosumnes "
Winnick, William	40	Holland	Farmer	Mud Springs "

NAME.	Age	Place of Nativity.	Occupation.	Local Residence.
Wiedman, John G. Fred'k.	33	Wirtemburg	Miner	Georgetown Township.
Whistler, William Girard	84	Pennsylvania	Cook	Diamond Spr'gs "
Webber, Joseph	37	Germany	Miner	Mud Springs "
White, James	28	Great Britain	"	" "
Wilson, James	48	Scotland	"	Placerville "
Welty, John	50	Switzerland	Hotel Keeper	" "
Woodward, William	34	Ireland	Farmer	White Oak "
Winstandley, Chas. War'n	47	Kentucky	Laborer	Lake Valley "
Wonn, Alex. Franklin	34	Maryland	Miner	Greenwood "
Wilson, William Thomas	37	Kentucky	Hosp'l Steward	Placerville "
Wilson, Charles	25	Ireland	Teamster	Mud Springs "
Wible, Daniel Franklin	29	Pennsylvania	Miner	Diamond Sp'gs "
Webster, Strawther Mat'n	45	Virginia	Farmer	" "
Wach, Belthasar	40	Switzerland	Miner	Coloma "
Wonderley, Alexander	21	Pennsylvania	Painter	Placerville "
Wuist, George	51	Germany	Miner	" "
Wilson, Owen	27	England	"	Georgetown "
Whisenant, Thomas	66	South Carolina	Butcher	" "
Watkins, Edmond Gardner	31	Kentucky	Shoemaker	" "
Wilton, Aretas James	37	New York	Farmer	" "
White, Charles Jay	54	Vermont	Shoemaker	" "
Wood, William Thomas	48	Dist. Columbia	Miner	" "
Wheedon, Zera	26	Indiana	Lumberman	Sly Park.
Williams, William Albert	35	Missouri	Miner	Pleasant Valley.
White, Richard Batson	26	Arkansas	"	Diamond Springs T'p.
Winne, Timothy	62	Ireland	"	Placerville Township.
Williams, James Lucian	40	New York	Farmer	Coloma "
Woodruff, Erastus	40	Connecticut	"	" "
Wagner, Wm. Wash'ton	41	Illinois	"	" "
Wilson, Robert Mills	52	Massachusetts	"	" "
Whitehead, Timothy	51	New Jersey	Carpenter	El Dorado.
West, Joseph C	32		Miner	Cosumnes Township.
Wells, Peter	24	Canada	Farmer	" "
Willson, Eskridg John	38	Kentucky	Miner	" "
Wilson, Egbert Livingston	34	Illinois	Farmer	White Oak "
Wentz, Alfred	35	Maryland	Miner	" "
Webb, John Brown	37	Ohio	Laborer	" "
Wesner, David	29	Illinois	Farmer	" "
Warson, Thomas	40	Missouri	Gunsmith	" "
Wagner, Henry Augustus	38	Canada	Miner	" "
While, James Blevins	29	Alabama	"	Kelsey "
Wyckoff, Dennis	46	New Jersey	"	" "
Warner, Marvin Lewis	42	New York	Shoemaker	Greenwood "
Williams, John Nicols	37	Massachusetts	Miner	" "
Withington, Sumner And.	36	Massachusetts	"	" "
Wood, John	46	New York	Farmer	" "
Wray, Geo. Washington	36	Indiana	"	Placerville "
Wilson, John	25	New York	Laborer	" "
Webb, William Weston	30	Texas	Miner	Mountain "
Ward, Ariel Herbert	27	Maine	"	" "
White, Joseph	44	Ohio	Farmer	Mud Springs "
Waggoner, William	26	Tennessee	Miner	" "
W kel, John	40	North Carolina	"	" "
W kel, George	36	North Carolina	"	" "
Warren, Harvey Elias	30	Maine	Jobber	Georgetown "
Wooley, Benjamin	33	Pennsylvania	Miner	" "
Woodworth, Lyman	35	New York	"	Sly Park.
Wiseman, And. Jackson	32	Pennsylvania	Teamster	" "
Wiltse, William	31	New York	Farmer	Placerville "
Wheeler, Riley	61	New Jersey	Laborer	" "
Williamson, Aaron	36	Indiana	Miner	" "
Williamson, Warren	47	Maine	Laborer	" "
Walrath, James W	32	Tennessee	Engineer	" "

NAME.	Age	Place of Nativity.	Occupation.	Local Residence.
Ward, Benj. Franklin	50	Massachusetts	Hotel-keeper	Placerville Township.
White, Caleb Arnold	43	Massachusetts	Miner	White Oak. "
Wallace, Thomas	32	Great Britain	Farmer	" "
Williams, George	47	Great Britain	Machinist	" "
Williams, Peter	39	Austria	Miner	Placerville "
Woods, John "W."	44	Ireland	Farmer	Kelsey "
Wingo, Joseph Henry	34	SouthCarolina	Miner	Mud Springs "
Wagner, John	38	Wirtemburg	"	Placerville "
Webster, Nelson	48	Kentucky	"	Mud Springs "
Weist, George	30	Pennsylvania	"	Georgetown "
Wing, Ezra	58	Massachusetts	"	" "
Wriston, Samuel Epthale.	32	Illinois	Dairyman	Lake Valley "
Warren, Job Ellis	33	Massachusetts	Cooper	" "
Wait, Franklin Andrews	33	Ohio	Miner	Salmon Falls "
Wood, Asahel Madison	32	New York	"	Greenwood "
Williams, Robert Noyce	55	Connecticut	Farmer	Placerville "
Waldron, William	45	Maine	Engineer	" "
Werntz, Gabriel	34	Pennsylvania	Blacksmith	Grizzly Flat.
Williams, Lewis	34	Missouri	Teamster	Cosumnes Township.
Williams, Jackson L	29	Ohio	Laborer	" "
Willson, John	36	Tennessee	Miner	" "
Wheeler, Noah "G."	35	New York	Wheelwright	Mud Springs "
Walker, John Thomas	58	Virginia	Laborer	" "
Williams, Leroy Freeman	34	Illinois	Farmer	" "
Watkins, William	59	Ohio	"	" "
Watkins, John William	23	Illinois	"	" "
Worth, Gideon	53	Massachusetts	"	" "
Welch, Levi	34	Tennessee	"	" "
Walker, George Burt	41	Vermont	Hostler	" "
Welch, James Nealy	24	Missouri	Laborer	" "
Wright, Edward Thomas	25	Great Britain	Miner	Placerville "
Waggner, John	48	Germany	"	Kelsey "
Wilt, William	42	France	"	Georgetown "
Wagner, Martin	38	Prussia	Merchant	Placerville "
Walker, Jabez Crocker	38	Ohio	Sawyer	Diamond Sp. "
Worthen, Alfred Marshal	33	Maine	Blacksmith	Placerville "
Wright, William	44	Vermont	Dairyman	" "
Woolher, Jurry	42	Germany	Miner	Salmon Falls "
Wirtz, Jacob	56	Switzerland	Farmer	Placerville "
Wilson, Franklin Fletcher	45	N. Hampshire	Laborer	" "
Whitacre, William Taylor	24	Ohio	Rancher	Lake Valley "
Walsh, Patrick	45	Great Britain	Miner	Placerville "
Wylie, Robert Henry	34	Great Britain	"	Brownsville.
Wertz, Casper	42	Switzerland	Farmer	Diamond Springs.
Williams, Harris Jerry	44	Pennsylvania	Miner	Placerville Township
Walker, Adolph Henry	39	Germany	"	Greenwood "
Watt, Peter	30	Great Britain	"	Placerville "
Whitmarsh, Thomas	45	Massachusetts	Farmer	" "
Wheeler, Sardine Gilson	31	Vermont	Miner	Georgetown "
Wakefield, Claudius B	52	New York	Farmer	" "
Worster, Geo. Augustus	38	Maine	Teamster	" "
Walz, John	31	Wirtemburg	Butcher	Mud Springs "
Woodward, Jas. Elliott	43	Ohio	Ranchman	Greenwood "
West, Wm. Franklin	26	Pennsylvania	Miner	Placerville "
Woodward, Edward	33	Great Britain	"	

Y

NAMES.	Age	Place of Nativity.	Occupation.	Local Residence.
Yoakum, Isaac	63	Tennessee	Farmer	Placerville Township.
Young, Commodore Perry	50	Tennessee	Miner	Coloma "
Yunglof, Jacob Frederick	47	Sweden	Gunsmith	Placerville "
Young, Orin Barton	44	New York	Stable-keeper	" "
Young, Jacob	33	Germany	Miner	White Oak "
Young, Thomas Kinman	32	Virginia	"	Diamond Sprg's "
Yount, John	53	Ohio	"	Indian Diggings.
Yeaden, Joshua	52	England	Blacksmith	Diamond Springs Tp
Yancey, Baylus	37	Georgia	Miner	Georgetown Township.
Young, Richard Samuel	31	Michigan	Laborer	Placerville "
Yarnold, Richard	36	Atlantic Ocean	Hotel-keeper	" "
Yarbrough, Chas. Trigg	49	Kentucky	Miner	" "
Young, Josiah Jordan	32	Maine	Teamster	Cosumnes "
Young, Nathan	50	Kentucky	Hotel-keeper	Mud Springs "
Younger, Thos. Anderson	31	North Carolina	Miner	Gold Hill.

Z

Zeip, Jacob	41	Bavaria	Brewer	Placerville Township.
Zener, George	33	Germany	Miner	" "
Zollar, Frederick	42	Ohio	"	Grizzly Flat.
Zellio, Francis	43	Switzerland	Dairyman	Placerville Township.
Zuisler, Charles	23	Ohio	Clerk	" "
Zentgraf, Jacob	46	Germany	Farmer	White Oak Township.
Zacher, Christ	47	Prussia	Tailor	Diamond Spr'gs "
Zerterfleth, Henry	33	Hanover	Miner	Mud Springs "
Zeller, John	50	Germany	"	" "
Zimmer, John	57	Bavaria	"	Diamond Spr'gs "
Zerga, Stefano	31	Italy	"	" "
Zearing, Jacob	42	Pennsylvania	Farmer	Georgetown "
Zumault, Isaiah	31	Missouri	Miner	Placerville "
Zeigler, Joseph	42	Baden	Farmer	" "
Zumault, Andrew Jackson	21	Missouri	Miner	" "
Zeigler, Wendeling	43	Germany	"	Greenwood "

State of California, } ss.
COUNTY OF EL DORADO.

I, D. W. Standeford, County Clerk of the County aforesaid, and ex-officio Clerk of the County Court, do hereby certify the foregoing to be a true and complete copy of the Great Register of El Dorado County.

In witness whereof, I hereunto set my hand and impress the Seal of said County Court, at office in the city of Placerville, this the 15th day of July, A. D. 1867.

D. W. STANDEFORD, Clerk.
By Aaron Bell, Deputy Clerk.

1868 Supplement

to the

Great Register of 1867

El Dorado County, California

GREAT REGISTER SUPPLEMENT.

EL DORADO COUNTY.

[A]

NAME.	Age.	Place of Nativity	Occupation.	Local Residence.
Aurelie, Chesti.	28	Switzerland	Miner	Georgetown Township.
Anderson, James Andrew	39	Norway	"	" "
Andrew, Thomas	52	Kentucky	"	" "
Alaxander, Re.	25	Switzerland	"	" "
Ambrose, John	49	N. Hampshire.	Laborer	Sacramento County.
Armstrong, William Thomas	35	Virginia	Miner	Placerville Township.
Alley, Zadock Fowler	29	Indiana	Telegr'h operator	" "
Allen, William	36	New York	Ship maker	Georgetown Township.
Anderson, Stephen	35	Tennessee	Miner	Mud Springs Township.
Atchison, Thomas Jefferson	53	Kentucky	Woodchopper	Salmon Falls Township.
Angove, James	41	Great Britain.	Miner	Placerville Township.
Allen, James Cochran	28	" "	Wheelwright	" "
Albricht, William Henry	41	Germany	Merchant	Diamond Springs Tp.
Arguelar, Domingo	28	Chile	Miner	Georgetown Township.
Avery, Alvin Devius	35	N. Hampshire.	Shake maker	Placerville Township.
Ayers, William Wallace	29	Iowa	Druggist	" "
Anderson, Joevgon	40	Denmark	Miner	Badger Hill.

B

Burk, James Laurence	28	Ireland	Miner	Georgetown Township.
Booth, Elijah	31	Kentucky	"	White Oak Township.
Bonfountinie Marcelle	50	Switzerland	"	Georgetown Township.
Borella, Abrams	27	"	Farmer	" "
Bertiori, Baul	34	"	"	Mud Springs Township.
Bramley, William	63	England	Hunter	" "
Beckman, Ludwig	43	Hanover	Miner	" "
Bronner, Battirta	25	Switzerland	"	Georgetown Township.
Batchelor, James Henry	38	England	"	Coloma Township.
Bull, Peter Frederick	40	Prussia	Hotel keeper	Placerville Township.
Barbee, Victor	40	France	Miner	Greenwood Township.
Baggini, Paolo	31	Switzerland	"	Kelsey Township.
Berta, Emanuel	28	"	"	Coloma Township.
Bischel, Anton	64	Bavaria	Farmer	" "
Bussinger, John	46	Wurtemberg.	Stone cutter	" "

SUPPLEMENT.

NAME.	Age	Place of Nativity	Occupation.	Local Residence.
Bond, William	48	Great Britain	Miner	Placerville Township.
Brindley, Joseph	38	" "	Blacksmith	" "
Boun, George Washington	48	New York	Stage driver	" "
Boswell, George Barnett	27	Indiana	Machinist	" "
Blacksher, Alen Green	45	Tennessee	Miner	Cosumnes Township.
Brannan, William	36	Ireland	Hotel keeper	Lake Valley Township.
Blinn, Huron	50	New York	Laborer	" "
Brandon, Edgar	38	Pennsylvania	Miner	White Oak Township.
Bendfeldt, Frederick	38	Germany	"	Placerville Township.
Bingham, Morgan Lewis	51	New York	"	Coloma Township.
Benjamin, De Witt Clinton	41	Connecticut	Millwright	Kelsey Township.
Birch, William Augustus	29	Michigan	Farmer	" "
Burrows, Elijah	26	Great Britain	Blacksmith	Placerville Township.
Blacklock, John	25	Great Britain	Miner	" "
Blight, John	45	Great Britain	"	Greenwood.
Bayless, John Marion	33	Ohio	"	"
Buel, Austin	43	New York	"	Placerville.
Bodfish, Russell Sturges	63	Massachusetts	"	Coloma Township.
Brown, Charles	38	Sweden	"	White Oak Township.
Barton, Hiram Emott	36	New York	Farmer	" "
Bearinger, Augustus	35	Germany	"	" "
Barney, George Washington	26	New York	"	Cosumnes Township.
Baker, Ira David	28	Ohio	Engraver	Diamond Township.
Bronson, Russell	42	Indiana	Farmer	Placerville Township.
Burdick, Jared Crandal	53	New York	Miner	" "
Bradford, William Henry	46	Vermont	"	Georgetown Township.
Benn, Peyton Wright	37	Missouri	"	Placerville.
Brown, William Henry	34	Ohio	Stable keeper	Mud Springs Township.
Babcock, Washington	35	Michigan	Miner	" "
Bird, Christopher	28	New York	Blacksmith	Mountain Township.
Brown, Charles Allen	30	Massachusetts	Miner	" "
Branthover, David	33	Pennsylvania	"	Kelsey Township.
Berack, William Thomas	21	Missouri	Teamster	Placerville Township.
Brice, George Washington	50	Kentucky	"	Cosumnes.
Brooks, Adam	35	Ohio	Miner	Placerville.
Behnke, August	21	Germany	"	"
Beilenberg, Paul Deiderick	54	Denmark	"	Kelsey Township.
Beker, Heman	54	Prussia	Farmer	Mud Springs Township.
Bainbridge, John George	43	Great Britain	Machinist	" "
Blacklock, William	34	Great Britain	Miner	Placerville.
Bick, Peter Nicholas	37	Denmark	"	Greenwood Township.
Buiff, Conrad Frederick	38	Germany	"	Salmon Falls.
Brown, William Henry	34	Kentucky	Teamster	Mud Springs.
Burr, Edwin Allen	44	Connecticut	Quartz miner	Mountain Township.
Brook, James Joseph	21	Illinois	Bridge tender	Coloma.
Brainard, William Nathan	21	New York	Clerk	Placerville.
Bell, Francis	29	Canada	Telegraph opera'r	Lake Valley.
Brune, Marco	35	Sardinia	Miner	Placerville.
Birch, George Washington	53	New York	Farmer	New Town.
Bolinger, Jacob	36	Bavaria	Butcher	Placerville.
Boyd, Samuel	39	Kentucky	Miner	Cosumnes.
Blair, Robert	29	Scotland	Hotel keeper	Sportsman's Hall.

C

NAME.	Age	Place of Nativity	Occupation.	Local Residence.
Charden, Stephen	50	France	Miner	Cosumnes Township.
Coellier, Pierrie	50	"	Cook	Georgetown.
Connell, William	44	Great Britain	Farmer	Diamond Springs.
Child, William	33	" "	Miner	Mud Springs Township.
Carroll, John	35	Vermont	"	Placerville.
Carpenter, John Calvin	35	New York	Farmer	Georgetown.
Christie, William	35	Canada	Blacksmith	Mud Springs.
Carlos, Henry	42	Pennsylvania	Miner	Placerville.
Calhoon, James	39	Ohio	Freight agent	"
Cooley, George Devaraux	39	Tennessee	Miner	Georgetown.

SUPPLEMENT.

NAME.	Age	Place of Nativity	Occupation.	Local Residence.
Churchill, James	30	Maine	Lawyer	Cosumnes.
Crossgrove, Charles Edwin	27	Delaware	Farmer	"
Carney, Chester	41	Pennsylvania	Farmer	Mud Springs.
Christens, Frederick	38	Germany	Miner	"
Cady, Thomas	36	"	Laborer	Placerville.
Coates, Benjamin Franklin	21	Wisconsin	Miner	Placerville Township.
Clements, James Edward	35	Virginia	Blacksmith	Mud Springs "
Cruss, William	42	Missouri	Miner	"
Crippin, James	21	Iowa	Clerk	Placerville.
Castle, William Dr.	43	New York	Hotel keeper	Lake Valley.
Castle, Isaac Nelson	21	Michigan	Butcher	"
Curley, James H	35	Massachusetts	Hotel waiter	Cosumnes.
Chappell, Joshua	36	New York	Teamster	Placerville.
Coupland, Benjamin Harrison	35	Virginia	Laborer	Shingle Springs.
Carter, George Henry	36	Kentucky	Lumberman	Sly Park.
Corvaniano, Joseph	25	Italy	Gardener	Placerville.
Cobetich, Paulo	34	Austria	Miner	Salmon Falls Township
Crovichich, Mateo	33	"	"	" "
Curtis, Francis Edwards	21	Ohio	Butcher	Greenwood "
Creighton, John Franklin	20	Maine	School teacher	Smith's Flat.
Couch, Jesse	46	United States	Supervisor	Latrobe.
Callegari, Sieten	35	Sardinia	Miner	Placerville.
Carpenter, W. General Jackson	20	Indiana	"	Kelsey Township.

D

NAME.	Age	Place of Nativity	Occupation.	Local Residence.
Diss, Paule	40	France	Miner	Diamond Springs Tp.
Dobbas, Elia	34	Switzerland	"	Georgetown Township.
Dotta, Godovico	23	"	"	" "
Dickerman, Benjamin, Jr.	41	Massachusetts	Quartz miner	Mud Springs "
Dornin, William	45	Ireland	Gardener	Placerville.
Drew, Martin	36	England	Harnessmaker	Diamond Springs Tp.
Dages, Mendell	38	Prussia	Miner	Georgetown "
David, John	39	"	"	Greenwood "
Duthman, Garhard Heinreich	33	Hanover	Engraver	Diamond Springs "
Doherty, James	83	Ireland	Gardener	Placerville. "
Doyal, Richard Henry	32	Louisiana	Tailor	" "
Dutton, Reuel William	24	Massachusetts	Teamster	Cosumnes "
Duple, Louis	25	Italy	Farmer	Placerville.
Davenport, Ezekiel Davenport	35	South Carolina	Miner	Diamond Springs.
Dean, Edward H	36	New York	"	Mud Springs.
Didway, John	30	Ohio	"	Mountain Township.
Duncan, John Gates	56	United States	Farmer	Salmon Falls.
Dick, Lewis Franklin	33	United States	Miner	Placerville.
Dean, Job Godfrey	53	Massachusetts	Farmer	Latrobe, Mud Spring Tp
Depovli, Antonio	37	Italy	Miner	Mud Springs Township
Danz, Girolmo	30	Switzerland	Dairyman	Placerville "
Deitrich, Nicholas	54	France	Miner	Mud Springs.
Davis, Edward Livingston	34	Nor. Carolina	Driver	Placerville.

E

NAME.	Age	Place of Nativity	Occupation.	Local Residence.
Ebat, Casper Joseph	23	Iowa	Butcher	Diamond Springs Tp.
Eugenio, Broner	40	Switzerland	Miner	Georgetown Township.
Ellen, Alfred	39	Hanover	"	Mud Springs "
Edwards, Aaron Alfred	22	Connecticut	Tinsmith	Placerville "
Edson, Curtis Platt	48	New York	Miner	" "
Easty, Henry	53	"	Teamster	"
Evins, John	48	Tennessee	Miner	Mud Springs.
Eaves, William	34	England	Jeweller	Georgetown.
Esinheart, Bartholomew	48	Great Britain	Miner	Cosumnes.
Eberstine, Charles	62	Germany	"	Mud Springs.
Edwards, John Robert	53	Great Britain	Surgeon	"
Eesman, Ludecirg	60	Germany	Carpenter	Placerville.

SUPPLEMENT.

NAME.	Age.	Place of Nativity	Occupation.	Local Residence.
Eddy, James Franklin	38	Rhode Island.	Miner	Mud Springs.
Erway, James	24	Michigan	Teamster	Shingle Springs.
Erway, Benjamin	26	"	"	" "
Edwards, John	36	Virginia	Blacksmith	" "
Egger, Jacob	32			

F

NAME.	Age.	Place of Nativity	Occupation.	Local Residence.
Fress, Frederick	21	Wurtemberg	Farmer	Placerville.
Fendley, Richard	38	South Carolina	Miner	White Oak.
Filippini, Rinaldo	26	Switzerland	Merchant	Georgetown.
Freeman, George Washington	22	Illinois	Farmer	White Oak.
Fyhn, Peter Hanson	38	Denmark	Miner	Greenwood.
Furguson, Charles Gardnor	26	Illinois	"	Placerville.
Fovina, Sadovico	31	Switzerland	"	Georgetown.
Forni, Samuel	34		"	"
Franklin, Joseph	32	Great Britain		Placerville.
Forman, Hambleton	41	Virginia	Farmer	Latrobe.
Farlender, John	47	Baden	Baker	Coloma.
Fields, Green	25	Illinois	Miner	Diamond Springs.
Fields, Jeremiah	55	Nor. Carolina	Farmer	" "
Forbs, Jothan Oscar	21	Ohio	Teamster	Georgetown.
Fradley, Robert	31	New York	Miner	Mud Springs.
Flyn, James	30	"	"	Placerville.
Fagan, John	40	Ireland	"	
Fowler, William James	40	Great Britain	"	Kelsey's.
Farati, Carle	21	Italy	"	Diamond Springs.
Francis, Isah Williams	32	Connecticut	Bookkeeper	White Oak.
Franklin, Edward	36	Ohio	Teamster	Diamond.
Frank, John	47	Austria	Miner	Placerville.
Fiori, Ercole	40	Italy	"	
Frakes, Jesse	48	Ohio	Laborer	Cosumnes.

G

NAME.	Age.	Place of Nativity	Occupation.	Local Residence.
Gavry, Edward	39	Great Britain	Miner	Grizzly Flat.
Gerard, Martin	32	France	"	Georgetown.
Guidico, Matale Rowerio	38	Switzerland	Blacksmith	"
Gosch, Peter	39	Denmark	Miner	Mud Springs.
Gerber, Heinrich	40	Baden	Farmer	"
Gillespie, Patrick	53	Ireland	Miner	"
Gedge, George	61	England	Master mariner	Grizzly Flat.
Goodman, George	39	Austria	Miner	"
Giovani, Toncla	61	Italy	"	Georgetown.
Grorivini, Gaitane	31	Switzerland	"	Kelsey's.
Grove, Henry	50	Tennessee	"	Placerville.
Gerkins, William	41	Prussia	"	Diamond Springs.
Grigg, Leonard	42	Ohio	Blacksmith	White Oak.
Gordon, Henry	36	Illinois	Teamster	Salmon Falls.
Givanini, Gacomo	33	Switzerland	Miner	Placerville.
Gerle, Christopher Cyrus	34	Sweden	Farmer	Coloma.
Glass, John	56	Illinois	Tailor	Georgetown.
George, Even Edward	35	Pennsylvania	Teamster	"
Goodridge, James Sumner	34	Maine	Farmer	Placerville.
George, Thomas	23	Great Britain	Miner	
Gay, Daniel, "N. D."	65	Virginia	Carpenter	Mud Springs.
Grant, Elizur	37	Connecticut	Miner	Placerville.
Gibson, Jonathan	34	Ohio	"	Diamond Springs.
Gray, William Thomas	24	Illinois	"	White Oak.
Garent, Cartlen	42	Denmark	Farmer	Diamond Springs.
George, Thomas Albert	46	Kentucky	Miner	Mud Springs.
Gilbert, George Hiern	43	New York	Artist	Placerville.
Giles, Oliver Merrill	21	Ohio	Teamster	Lake Valley.
Gibson, Jonathan	34	Ohio	Laborer	Lake Valley.

SUPPLEMENT.

NAME.	Age.	Place of Nativity	Occupation.	Local Residence.
Gilman, Albert Mason	27	United States	Miner	Mountain.
Gilmore, Henry Harrison	26	Maine	"	Placerville.
Geamboni, Antoni	37	Switzerland	"	Mud Springs.
Gottlieb, Julius	37	Denmark	"	Grizzly Flat.
Grundy, James	50	Great Britain	Farmer	Mud Springs.
Gray, Ensley Taylor	21	Illinois		White Oak.
Gruebler, Salomon	35	Switzerland	Miner	Salmon Falls.
Glynn, Frederick Wallace	33	New York	Dentist	Placerville.
German, John	25	Austria	Miner	Salmon Falls.
Goddard, Samuel Richardson	40	New York	Laborer	Placerville.
Galpin, Curtis	40	Ohio	Miner	American Valley.
Gobble, Obediah	26	Nor. Carolina	"	Diamond Springs.

H

NAME.	Age.	Place of Nativity	Occupation.	Local Residence.
Hannay, Andrew	27	Scotland	Miner	Georgetown.
Holmon, Charles	41	Sweden	"	"
Hennisy, James	44	Ireland	Laborer	Greenwood Township.
Hoffman, Harvey	37	Hanover	Miner	"
Hansen, John Frederick Peter	35	Denmark	Miner	"
Henrig, George	45	Bavaria	Stone mason	Coloma.
Heenan, James	36	Ireland	Laborer	Placerville.
Huftab, Peter	36	New York	Miner	"
Hagedon, James Knox	24	Wisconsin	Teamster	"
Haas, Henry	46	Nassau	Miner	Diamond Springs.
Holworson, Holwor	38	Sweden	"	Placerville.
Humson, Patrick	45	Great Britain	"	Cosumnes Township.
Holman, Michael	27	Germany	Teamster	
Holman, James Hawthorn	31	Indiana		Cosumnes Township.
Hart, Thomas Henry	52	Ireland	Miner	Latrobe.
Hunt, William	28	Hamburg	Laborer	Placerville.
Hammon, Elisha Benson	46	Maine	Teamster	Mud Springs.
Hoar, Charles Augustus	27	"	Farmer	Cosumnes.
Holland, James	28	Ireland	Miner	"
Hittman, Joseph	25	Prussia	"	"
Howe, Joseph	25	England	Farmer	White Oak.
Haase, Peter	36	Germany	"	Grizzly Flat.
Hays, Cicero	29	Ohio	Livery stable keep	Placerville.
Hunt, Boswell Chapin	23	Vermont	Miner	Mud Springs.
Hart, Charles	61	Connecticut	Farmer	"
Hawkins, Harland Powers	50	New York	Teamster	"
Hall, Richard Henry	35	Maine	Miner	"
Holloway, Henry	29	Rhode Island	Shake maker	Placerville.
Henry, Thomas	63	Tennessee	Farmer	Mountain.
Hammond, James	42	Kentucky	Miner	"
Houseworth, Benja'n Winslow	39	Virginia	"	Salmon Falls.
Houston, Noah Beales	39	Maine	Mechanic	Lake Valley.
Hall, William Alexander	36	New York	Miner	Mud Springs.
Holmes, John	36	Vermont	Laundryman	Placerville.
Holden, Abraham	52	England	Miner	White Oak.
Harny, Thomas	45	Great Britain	"	Kelsey.
Hulford, Edward Wilkins	30	" "	"	Georgetown.
Heeguard, Sophus	37	Denmark	"	Placerville.
Hosking, Solomon Pierce	23	England	"	Mountain Township.
Harsha, Samuel	37	Ireland	Packer	White Oak.
Hugill, George Washington	25	Wisconsin	Miner	Placerville.
Hans, Abraham	39	France	Merchant	"
Harris, John	54	Kentucky	Milling & Mining	Shingle Springs.
Hickey, William Swaney	29	Missouri	Laborer	Cosumnes Township.
Howard, Mark Elery	25	Illinois		
Hukins, James	27	New York	Laborer	Cosumnes Township.
Ham, George Franklin	52	N. Hampshire	Shoemaker	Placerville.

NAME	Age	Place of Nativity	Occupation	Local Residence
Illig, Morris	42	Saxony	Druggist	El Dorado.
Iverson, Ives	27	Norway	Farmer	White Oak.
Irving, James	42	Ireland	Miner	Mud Springs.
Ingersoll, Owen	61	New York	Farmer	Diamond Springs.
Ivanis, Piajo	33	Austria	Miner	Salmon Falls.

J

NAME	Age	Place of Nativity	Occupation	Local Residence
Jesko, August	30	Prussia	Farmer	Mud Springs.
Julius, Jean Adolph	81	Germany	Miner	Greenwood.
Jager, August		Prussia	"	Coloma.
Junglas, Conrad	48	Hesse Cassel	"	Greenwood.
Jones, James	27	New York	"	Coloma.
Jeffers, Isaac George	40	Ireland	Carpenter	Smith's Flat.
Johnson, William Jackson	52	Massachusetts	Travel'ng lecturer	White Oak.
Johnson, Henry Martin	36	New York	Clerk	Mud Springs.
Johansen, Christian	39	Denmark	Miner	Coloma.
Jameson, Joseph	51	Pennsylvania	"	Cosumnes.
Johnson, Dennis	33	New York	Dairyman	Lake Valley.
Jameson, John McKnight	63	Virginia	Farmer	Cosumnes.
Jackson, Thomas	49	Sweden	Miner	Georgetown.
James, Jeffery	34	England	"	Placerville.
Johnson, Milon	21	Canada	"	"
Jantzan, August	34	Hanover	Saloon keeper	" 1st Ward.
Johnson, William	35	Great Britain	Miner	Georgetown.

K

NAME	Age	Place of Nativity	Occupation	Local Residence
Kind, Henry	26	Germany	Merchant	Georgetown.
Kyburg, Samuel	57	Switzerland	Farmer	White Oak.
Kasselring, Adam	96	Germany	Gardener	Coloma.
Kincheloe, George	41	Virginia	Baker	Placerville.
Knapp, Nathaniel Warren	27	New York	Teamster	Mud Springs.
Kohn, Jacob	49	Austria	Merchant	Placerville.
Keouss, Frederick	56	Germany	Miner	White Oak.
Kelley, Michael	37	Ireland	"	Placerville.
Knudson, Frank	30	Denmark	"	White Oak.
Kohlert, John	35	"	"	Cosumnes.
Keller, George Washington	77	Pennsylvania	"	White Oak.
Klaphake, Johann Heinrich	38	Germany	"	Salmon Falls.
Kay, William	50	England	"	Shingle Springs.
Kendall, John	21	Maine	Teamster	Cosumnes.

L

NAME	Age	Place of Nativity	Occupation	Local Residence
Loage, Michael	48	Ireland	Miner	Coloma.
Lunce, Joshua Witts	38	Kentucky	"	Placerville.
Loomis, George Allen	54	Massachusetts	Farmer	Coloma.
Lebar, Conrad Jackson	34	New York	Miner	Georgetown.
Laners, Nicolas	38	Holland	Farmer	Cosumnes.
Lipp, Joseph	28	Missouri	Miner	Mud Springs.
Lewis, Henry	29	Louisiana	Chief cook	Placerville.
Lebe, Daniel	38	Ohio	Miner	"
Laphiew, James Edward	30	Alabama	"	Latrobe.
Luse, John	41	Pennsylvania	"	Placerville.
Letcher, James Wilber	47	New York	Farmer	"
Lobden, Henry	33	Hanover	Miner	White Oak.
Larsen, Nels Theodore Emil	41	Sweden & Nor.	Farmer	Placerville.
Lee, Thomas Francis	29	Ireland	Miner	Georgetown.
Larkin, Samuel	55	Pennsylvania	Laborer	Mud Springs.
Lanston, Joseph Van Pelt	42	Maryland	Miner	Lake Valley.
Lobronzen, Hennrick		Denmark	"	Greenwood.
Lioni, Filippo	42	Switzerland	Farmer	Placerville.

SUPPLEMENT.

NAME.	Age	Place of Nativity	Occupation.	Local Residence.
Lobry, John Henry	31	Kentucky	Pattern maker	Coloma.
Leiser, John	34	Germany	Laborer	Placerville.
Livingston, Rinald Rinaldini	24	Massachusetts	Polyphonist	White Rock Cañon.
Lewis, William A	39	Sweden	Miner	
Littlefield, Albert	34	Maine	Laborer	
Lewis, Charles Henry	29	N. Hampshire	Blacksmith	Placerville.

M

Miller, Moses	51	Ohio	Blacksmith	Placerville.
McCammin, Charles Carle	34	Illinois	Miner	"
Marsh, Janson Cooper	36	Pennsylvania	Farmer	"
Moore, George	40	Vermont	Laborer	White Oak.
McCreery, Alexander	45	Pennsylvania	"	"
Mitchell, Daniel Harvey	41	Virginia	Miner	Placerville.
Mock, Adam Alexander	36	N. Carolina	"	Georgetown.
McColloh, John	34	Ohio	Farmer	
Morgan, Frank	33	Great Britain	Miner	Greenwood.
Munzin, Francis	38	France	"	"
Moussees, Henry	28	Hanover	"	Cosumnes.
Moser, Frederick	48	N. Carolina	Farmer	Placerville.
McGhee, Andrew Jackson	31	Illinois	Miner	"
McArthur, Donald	39	New York	Teamster	Mud Springs.
Moon, Charles James	30	New York	Miner	Georgetown.
Marsh, Orlando Marble	28	Maine	Teamster	Salmon Falls.
Myers, Jeremiah Cylman	30	New York	Miner	Mud Springs.
McCartney, William	34	Indiana	Farmer	"
Meek, Jeremiah Robert	21	Illinois	Laborer	Placerville.
Mathews, William Thomas	51	Wales	Miner	
Marsh, Archibald	33	New York	Carpenter	Cosumnes.
Morey, Henry Sylvester	28	Maine	Machinist	Placerville.
McAfee, Angus Dudley	35	Canada	Miner	Cosumnes.
Marson, William "R"	34	Russia	Clerk	Diamond Township.
Marple, William Lewis	40	Pennsylvania	Artist	Placerville.
McGregor, William	49	Scotland	Farmer	"
Miller, Ed. Christian Gustave	34	Bavaria	Farmer	Diamond Springs.
Michaels, Fritz	49	Prussia	Gardener	Placerville.
McGrath, John	38	Ireland	Miner	Cosumnes.
McWilliam, John	29	Pennsylvania	"	Mud Springs.
Marcott, Adolph	44	Canada	"	Cosumnes.
Milliken, George Emery	38	Maine	Millwright	White Oak.
McDonald, Edward "A"	35	Scotland	Lumberman	Coloma.
McNiell, Charles	33	Ireland	Farmer	Mud Springs.
Mooney, Barney	35	Germany	Miner	"
Martin, Brewsie	31	Ohio	"	Georgetown.
Miller, John	31	Austria	"	Placerville.
McConnaba Battson Herald	21	Illinois	Teamster	"
Marrs, William	39	Arkansas	Miner	Cosumnes.
Moseley, Thomas James	32	Missouri	"	Nashville.
Miller, John Wesley	21	Indiana	"	Mud Springs.
McConkey, Hugh Brown	21	Ohio	Farmer	Placerville.
McGonagle, Joseph Barker	38	New York	Clerk	"
Mattoni Batista	32	Switzerland	Miner	Diamond Springs Tp.
Mayland, George Washington	38	Ohio	"	Cosumnes.
McNaughten, "F" Leger	44	Ohio	Carpenter	"
McKenna, William	38	Ireland	Miner	Placerville.

SUPPLEMENT.

NAME.	Age.	Place of Nativity	Occupation.	Local Residence.
Nichols, Eli Norton	33	New York	Clerk	Placerville.
North, Edwin Charles	41	New York	Miner	Cosumnes.
Nye, James Freeman	36	Maine	"	Mud Springs.
Noaks, James Thomas	30	Missouri	Blacksmith	Georgetown.
Neely, James Stewart	38	Mississippi	Miner	White Oak.
Nail, K. James	21	Iowa	Laborer	Mud Springs.
Nemcia, José	33	Mexico	Miner	Placerville.
Newell, Henry	51	Pennsylvania	Farmer	Cosumnes.

O

Orelli, Agostiono	31	Switzerland	Miner	Georgetown.
Orelli, Carlo	31	Switzerland	Carpenter	"
Orr, David	34	Delaware	Miner	Lake Township.
Orr, Alexander	32	Delaware	"	"
Odgers, John	41	England	"	"
Odgers, Samuel	23	Pennsylvania	"	Mud Springs.
Odgers, Henry	22	Pennsylvania	"	"
Odgers, Joseph	24	Pennsylvania	Engineer	"
Oslen, Hans Christian	47	Norway	Miner	Kelsey Township.
O'Farrell, James	30	Iowa	"	Mud Springs.
Oettinger, John	24	Germany	Butcher	

P

Parsons, George	41	Ireland	Miner	Coloma Township.
Parkhurst, William	36	Vermont	Teamster	Georgetown "
Pratt, William Henry	36	Massachusetts	Miner	"
Parry, Moninton K. Lewis	56	England	Steward	Diamond Springs Tp.
Pohll, Frederick	41	Prussia	Miner	Greenwood Township.
Peachey, William	35	Great Britain	"	Coloma.
Porter, Louis	35	Switzerland	"	Cosumnes Township.
Paddock, James L	25	Illinois	Clerk	"
Picoli, Baldisaro	40	Switzerland	Farmer	Diamond Springs Tp.
Pillman, William	36	Ohio	Teamster	" " "
Patton, Thomas Brinton	46	New York	Pub. Administr'tor	Placerville.
Phelps, Charles	35	Vermont	Laundryman	"
Pierce, William	51	"	Carpenter	"
Paraci, Julian	45	Mexico	Miner	Grizzly Flat.
Pini, Giovanni	43	Switzerland	Saloonkeeper	Georgetown.
Padrini, Giovani	35	"	Miner	
Pearson, John McFarlane	40	Scotland	Ice merchant	Placerville.
Powell, William	56	New York	Farmer	Mud Springs Township.
Peacock, Franklin Benjamin	47	Pennsylvania	"	Salmon Falls "
Pavey, George Andrews	21	New York	Clerk	Mud Springs "
Pepers, Edmond Thomas	23	Massachusetts	Dairyman	Lake Valley "
Patitaca, Marco	30	Austria	Miner	Salmon Falls "
Peters, Jonas	34	Ohio	"	Shingle Springs.
Papa, Aquilino	38	Switzerland	"	Diamond Springs Tp
Porter, Andrew Jackson	36	Maine	Farmer	Cosumnes "
Pearce, William	52	Georgia	Miner	" "
Pirs, Augustus	49	Louisiana	"	Pleasant Valley.

Q

Queen, John	45	Tennessee	Farmer	Mud Springs Township.

SUPPLEMENT.

NAME.	Age.	Place of Nativity	Occupation.	Local Residence.
Rohlfing, Frederick	38	Hanover	Storekeeper	White Oak Township.
Read, William Henry	44	New York	Miner	Georgetown "
Robertson, William	38	"	Engineer	" "
Rave, John	48	Chile	Miner	" "
Rosnasky, Kasimir	57	Russia	"	Mud Springs "
Razeullat, Jean	40	France	"	Greenwood "
Rossotto, Antonio	26	Switzerland	"	Kelsey "
Richardson, David Mansfield	48	Maine	"	Cosumnes "
Richardson, Williams Gaines M	21	Missouri	"	" "
Redman, William	57	New Jersey	Blacksmith	" "
Robinson, Horatio Loomis	35	New York	Miner	Placerville.
Richardson, Lorenzo Dow	47	N. Hampshire	"	Mud Springs Township.
Reed, Chauncey	50	Ohio	Farmer	" "
Ross, A. J.	38	New York	Teamster	" "
Raspberry, Phillip	41	Georgia	Miner	Cosumnes
Rhoads, Abraham	48	Pennsylvania	Stone mason	Placerville.
Rees, Thomas Benjamin	46	Wales	Carpenter	"
Reichard, Christian Ernst	39	Germany	Stagedriver	Coloma.
Rosetta, Martin	42	Switzerland	Miner	Kelsey Township.
Roseti, Petri	39	"	"	" "
Rust, George	47	Virginia	"	Mud Springs "
Roberts, William Harris	46	New York	Physician	Placerville "
Rice, Nathan Pickett	36	Kentucky	Teamster	"
Robbins, Gardner Juan	23	Vermont	Miner	Georgetown Township.
Rault, August	44	France	"	Brownsville.
Robertson, David Barclay	21	Scotland	Gardener	Placerville.

S

NAME.	Age.	Place of Nativity	Occupation.	Local Residence.
Stanivitch, Michael	36	Austria	Miner	Mountain Township.
Strecker, William	45	Denmark	"	Coloma "
Smith, John	65	England	Seaman	Georgetown "
Story, DeWitt Clinton	43	New York	Miner	Placerville "
Shivers, Benjamin	51	Georgia	"	Georgetown "
Stafford, Eugene	30	Ireland	"	Cosumnes "
Sims, James Maloy	45	Georgia	"	Placerville "
Steadman, Christ'her Potter, Jr	35	Rhode Island	"	Diamond Springs "
Scott, William Proctor	51	Massachusetts	Merchant	" " "
Slocum, Milton	31	Rhode Island	Clerk	Mud Springs "
Sherman, George Arthur	23	New York	Farmer	" "
Stephens, Joseph	63	Kentucky	Carpenter	" "
Sullivan, Burton	65	Delaware	Laborer	" "
Smith, Hiram A	37	New York	Teamster	" "
Stevans, Erastus	26	Ohio	"	" "
Smiley, Hyram Alexander	49	Maine	Machinist	Mountain "
Scott, John	21	Pennsylvania	Miner	Placerville "
Sepers, Lucas	37	Austria	"	" "
Snider, George	24	Ohio	"	" "
Stamper, Andrew Jackson	25	"	Tollkeeper	"
Senone, Ziehard	27	Switzerland	Blacksmith	Newtown.
Schmetyen, Bernhard	46	Prussia	Miner	White Oak Township.
Scolari, Basilio	35	Switzerland	"	Kelsey "
Simmins, Charles Cook	26	Massachusetts	Laborer	Mud Springs "
Savage, Jasper Hazen	27	Vermont	Miner	Placerville "
Snedaker, Samuel Blair	55	United States	Hotel keeper	White Oak "
Smith, William Dutra	33	Portugal	Storekeeper	Salmon Falls "
Silva, Joseph	33	Portugal	Miner	Greenwood "
Shoup, Simon	34	Ohio	Teamster	Placerville.
Spong, Samuel Wilcomb	41	Maryland	Miner	White Oak Township.
Settle, Joseph Morgan	48	Kentucky	"	Placerville "
Smith, Alfred Lindsley	24	Canada	Artist	"
Sipp, Joseph	28	Missouri	Miner	El Dorado.
Stintson, Daniel Alexander	36	Illinois	Farmer	Placerville.
Stewart, William	45	Scotland	Miner	Smith's Flat.

SUPPLEMENT.

NAME.	Age.	Place of Nativity	Occupation.	Local Residence.
Shaw, William	44	Illinois	Miner	Placerville.
Stewart, Albert Gallatin	39	Pennsylvania	Telegraph agent	"
Sturiza, Pietro	25	Austria	Miner	Salmon Falls Township.
Salcovich, George	38	"	"	" "
Selleck, Peters John	21	Illinois	"	Placerville.
Sittlefus, Albert	34	Maine	Laborer	"
Smith, August	46	Hamburg	Miner	Shingle Springs.
Sawer, Albert	21	Maine	Farmer	Cosumnes Township.
Simins, Emil	21	Germany	Clerk	Placerville.

T

Tinnetti, Carlo	34	Switzerland	Miner	Georgetown Township.
Ten Eyoh, Samuel	31	New York	"	Placerville.
Town, Henry Augustus	32	Maine	Carpenter	"
Taber, Frederick Ketchum	32	New York	Miner	Cosumnes Township.
Tusker, James Franklin	47	Vermont	Teamster	Lake Valley Township.
Teuscher, John, Jr	21	Ohio	Miner	Coloma.
Turner, Absolum	37	Tennessee	"	Mud Springs Township.
Tripp, Harvey Green	52	Rhode Island	"	" "
True, Warren	43	New York	"	Placerville.
Tobner, Charles	34	Hanover	Farmer	Coloma Township.
Tennis, James	23	Illinois	"	White Oak Township.
Tibbott, William	47	Iowa	"	Near El Dorado.
Tripp, Peleg	57	Rhode Island	Miner	Mud Springs Township.
Twiggs, Milton	50	Virginia	Teamster	" "
Teare, Philip	43	New York	Lawyer	" "
Taylor, Charles William	33	Arkansas	Miner	Placerville.
Tufel, Louis	48	Germany	"	Kelsey Township.
Tomlin, Orson Preston	30	Missouri	Laborer	Placerville.
Tarr, Warner, "F"	27	Maine	Engineer	Cosumnes Township.

V

Valli Carlo	37	Switzerland	Miner	Georgetown Township.
Vanderbilt, John Henry	39	New York	Hotel keeper	Placerville.
Vaughn, Alphonse Hyman	27	Rhode Island	"	"
Voss, William	38	Prussia	Farmer	Diamond Springs.
Verrinder, George	32	England	"	Mud Springs Township.
Verrinder, Henry	34	England	"	" "
Vail, Augustus Elliott	43	Maine	Miner	" "
Valentine, Peter Anthony	36	Great Britain	Farmer	Georgetown Township.
Vaugh, Ephraim	48	Ohio	Carpenter	Placerville.
Vosburg, Frank Butler	40	New York	Farmer	Garden Valley.

W

Williams, Frank	37	France	Miner	Placerville Township.
Wangler, Andrew	31	Baden	Lumberman	Diamond Springs
Wilkes, Philip Smith	41	Kentucky	Lumberman	Cosumnes Township.
White, James Albert	32	Maine	Laborer	Mud Springs Township.
Williams, Martin	41	Great Britain	Miner	" "
Westover, Frederick William	24	Missouri	"	" "
Wilson, William Jackson	42	Arkansas	"	" "
Williams, John Ruffin	26	Michigan	"	" "
Wilson, Daniel	36	Virginia	Saloon keeper	Mountain Township.
Williams, John	61	Kentucky	Farmer	Salmon Falls Township.
Woodworth, James Dennison	43	Massachusetts	Engineer	Mud Springs Township.
Woolever, Abram	45	Pennsylvania	Farmer	" "
Westour, William Frederick	23	Missouri	Miner	" "
Wright, Henry Allen	41	N. Hampshire	Carpenter	Placerville.
Wright, Sylvester	53	New York	Teamster	"
Witten, John Grant	33	Tennessee	Miner	Placerville Township.
West, Eugene	24	Baltic Ocean	Teamster	Diamond Springs

SUPPLEMENT.

NAME.	Age	Place of Nativity	Occupation.	Local Residence.
Wiegandt, Louis	28	Prussia	Miner	Grizzly Flat.
Wilson, Andrew Jackson	36	Ohio	Saloon keeper	Fairplay.
Watson, Andrew	47	Sweden	Miner	Latrobe.
Wilder, Edward Martin	35	Ohio	Teamster	Greenwood.
Wiseman, Jonathan Burton	37	Missouri	Miner	Mud Springs Township.
Wear, John Haywood	43	Indiana	Blacksmith	Georgetown Township.
Wood, Nathan Parkhurst	37	Maine	Miner	" "
Wentz, Jeremiah	41	Maryland	Teamster	Mud Springs Township.
Wagner, Thomas Milo	31	Canada	Miner	White Oak Township.
Whitman, George	62	S. Carolina	"	" "
Wade, Hampton Peters	42	Tennessee	"	Georgetown Township.
Wood, Lucas Arden	53	New York	Millwright	Mountain Township.
Wangler, Antonio	28	Baden	Farmer	Diamond Springs Tp.
Walk, James Addison	35	N. Carolina	"	" " "
William, James	23	Wisconsin	Laborer	Cosumnes Township.
Williams, Henry Perry	28	Indiana	Clerk	Placerville Township.
Woolfolk, Coleman Chaply	21	Missouri	Laborer	Cosumnes Township.

Y

Youer, Mathius	37	Germany	Miner	Georgetown Township.
Young, Henry William	22	Iowa	Farmer	

STATE OF CALIFORNIA,
   COUNTY OF EL DORADO. } ss.

I, W. N. *Muffley*, *County Clerk of the County aforesaid, and ex officio Clerk of the County Court, do hereby certify the foregoing to be a true and complete supplemental copy of the Great Register of El Dorado County.*

In witness whereof I hereunto set my hand and impress the seal of said County Court, at office in the City of Placerville, this the 31st day of August, A. D. 1868.

                                               W. N. MUFFLEY, *Clerk.*

www.ingramcontent.com/pod-product-compliance
Lightning Source LLC
Chambersburg PA
CBHW080252170426
43192CB00014BA/2660